FRAMEBREAK

Ian I. Mitroff

Richard O. Mason

Christine M. Pearson

FRAME BREAK

THE RADICAL

REDESIGN

OF AMERICAN

BUSINESS

Jossey-Bass Publishers
San Francisco

Substantial discounts on bulk quantities of Jossey-Bass books are available to corporations, professional associations, and other organizations. For details and discount information, contact the special sales department at Jossey-Bass Inc., Publishers. (415) 433-1740; Fax (415) 433-0499.

For sales outside the United States, contact Maxwell Macmillan International Publishing Group, 866 Third Avenue, New York, New York 10022.

Manufactured in the United States of America. Nearly all Jossey-Bass books and jackets are printed on recycled paper containing at least 10 percent postconsumer waste, and many are printed with either soy- or vegetable-based ink, which emits fewer volatile organic compounds during the printing process than petroleum-based ink.

Library of Congress Cataloging-in-Publication Data

Mitroff, Ian I.
    Framebreak : the radical redesign of American business / Ian
I. Mitroff, Richard L. Mason, Christine M. Pearson.
      p.   cm. — (The Jossey-Bass management series)
    Includes bibliographical references and index.
    ISBN 1-55542-606-9
    1. Industrial management—United States. 2. Organizational
behavior—United States. I. Mason, Richard O. II. Pearson,
Christine M. III. Title. IV. Series.
HD70.U5M54 1994
658—dc20
                                              93-42749
                                                  CIP

FIRST EDITION
HB Printing   10 9 8 7 6 5 4 3 2 1   *Code 9441*

The Jossey-Bass
Management Series

Consulting Editors
Organizations and Management

Warren Bennis
University of Southern California

Richard O. Mason
Southern Methodist University

Ian I. Mitroff
University of Southern California

CONTENTS

[A]s an old proverb has it: whom the gods want to destroy they send forty years of success. For a business theory is not a law of nature. Eventually it becomes inappropriate to the realities of the market and technology.

. . . The diagnosis is fairly simple. Whenever a business keeps on going downhill despite massive spending and heroic efforts by its people, the most likely cause is the obsolescence of its business theory.

—Peter Drucker

PREFACE

The predicament facing American business today is captured well in the opening lines of A. A. Milne's *Winnie the Pooh*. Christopher Robin is dragging his stuffed bear, Winnie, down a flight of stairs by his foot. With every step, Winnie's head is banging against a stair. As this is happening, he is saying to himself, "If only my head would stop hurting for a while, then maybe I could figure out a better way of coming down the stairs."

A similar refrain is heard today from American business: if only we could take a breather, a short time-out. If only the competition would let up for a while so we could catch our breath and regroup. If only we faced one less crisis, then perhaps we could figure out how to respond to the overwhelming forces threatening to crush us. If only . . . Unfortunately, things aren't letting up, nor does it look like they're going to.

Nearly all of the tactics that American business has tried in order to "stop its head from hurting" have failed or even made its problems worse. It has slashed budgets, cut departments, added departments, engaged in drastic work force reductions, forced early retirements, brought in motivational speakers, moved offshore, outsourced, and more. While many of these actions are necessary, and even help for a while, they do not recognize or respond to the real problem.

Nor is it accurate or helpful to attribute the problems that American organizations are facing to a temporary downturn in the economy. Such a view would have us believe that America's organizations are basically sound, and that once economic conditions right themselves, American organizations will be able to compete effectively again.

The real problem is that the basic structure of American business has outlived its usefulness. The difficulties that some of America's largest organizations (General Motors, IBM, Sears) have experienced recently are a vivid testament to the fact that the organizations of the nineteenth and early twentieth centuries are obsolete. They fail on two major counts: (1) the traditional functions around which they have largely been structured cannot handle the complex, systemic issues of today's world, and (2) the traditional structure not only ignores basic human needs but also demeans them.

Traditional organizations have lost their way. They no longer hear the "voices" of their various constituents and markets. They are unable to accumulate the kinds of knowledge and information they need in order to perform effectively. They are no longer in touch with their members' emotional needs. They no longer channel their organizational resources and energy toward their operations in an optimal way. And, for the most part, they no longer have a vision of their place in society and the larger world. As a result, many modern organizations are adrift in a sea of complexity, frustration, and change.

While quick fixes may provide short-term remedies, in the long run they only exacerbate the problem further. They do not constitute a strategy for responding to the true forces prompting change. In short, fine-tuning the current structure of American business will no longer suffice. Nothing less than a radical reconceptualization, a break from the old frame, is required.

An Invitation to Consider the Whole

Unlike the vast array of current management books that propose piecemeal solutions to the problems of organizational obsolescence, *Framebreak* invites corporate executives to step back from pressing everyday concerns to consider the larger picture and the longer view. In this way, it aims to help executives make real sense of the difficulties they regularly face. It proposes a radical new basis for restructuring American business: a philosophy of total ethical management.

This philosophy acknowledges the reality that today's world is complex and its issues are interdependent. It suggests that organizations have certain fundamental moral and ethical responsibilities to serve humanity's broader needs and to take seriously the emotional complexities of the people in organizations. Only when the structure of an organization reflects these responsibilities will the organization survive and thrive in this time of unprecedented challenge and opportunity.

Framebreak proposes that an organizational structure geared to today's (and tomorrow's) realities encompasses four essential dimensions: (1) knowledge and learning, (2) recovery and development, (3) world service and spirituality, and (4) world-class operations. These dimensions cut across the traditional functional lines to embrace complex, systemic issues and address the real needs of people in organizations. Along with six new key functions that we outline, they put into practice the proposition that successful business is an ethical enterprise.

Although we suggest where resources need to be allocated in the organization of the future, we refrain from specifying exactly how they should be allocated. This will vary from organization to organization, depending on its history, strengths, and weaknesses. Thus, we leave the details of implementation to those who know a particular organization most intimately. Instead, we provide a guiding vision to energize the quest for a new organizational form that will serve us in the twenty-first century and beyond.

The Journey Ahead

The eight chapters of *Framebreak* build, step-by-step, a new and radically different vision of tomorrow's organizations.

Chapter One looks at the outmoded structure of mod-

ern organizations and questions the assumptions underlying that structure. It discusses why that structure is no
longer functional and gives examples of organizations that
have begun experimenting with new forms to meet today's
challenges.

Chapter Two looks in detail at the dimensions of the
complex world surrounding business today and suggests
the broad outlines of a new organizational form designed
to cope with complexity.

Chapters Three through Six discuss in turn each of the
four essential dimensions of a new organizational design:
knowledge and learning, recovery and development,
world service and spirituality, and world-class operations.

Chapter Seven outlines a twelve-step approach to the
radical change that will be necessary for the realization of
total ethical management and the survival of organizations.

Chapter Eight explores the principles of total ethical
management that underlie the new functions and structure we have proposed and discusses how these principles
look in practice.

Acknowledgments

No book is ever the product of a single mind. The people
who have influenced *Framebreak* are too numerous to
mention by name. However, we especially want to single
out two of our closest friends and colleagues: C. West
Churchman and Warren Bennis. They deserve special mention because they have provided a constant source of inspi-

ration. We also wish to acknowledge the fine editorial advice and efforts of Lorraine Anderson and Cedric Crocker. Finally, Bill Hicks has been not only a strong and constant supporter of our work at Jossey-Bass but, most important of all, a good friend.

January 1994

IAN I. MITROFF
Los Angeles, California

RICHARD O. MASON
Dallas, Texas

CHRISTINE M. PEARSON
Chapel Hill, North Carolina

THE AUTHORS

Ian I. Mitroff is Harold Quinton Distinguished Professor of Business Policy and founder/director of the Center for Crisis Management, Graduate School of Business, University of Southern California. He received his B.S. degree (1961) in engineering physics, his M.S. degree (1963) in structural mechanics, and his Ph.D. degree (1967) in engineering science and philosophy of social science, all from the University of California, Berkeley.

Mitroff has consulted widely with major public and private organizations. He is a member of the American Association for the Advancement of Science, the Academy of Management, the American Psychological Association, the American Sociological Association, the Philosophy of Science Association, and the Institute for Management Science. He was president of the International Society for the Systems Sciences in 1992–1993.

Mitroff is author of fifteen books on business policy, corporate culture, managerial psychology and psychiatry, strategic planning, and philosophy and sociology of science. He has appeared on numerous radio and television programs, including "Financial News Network," "Window on Wall Street," and Michael Jackson's nationally syndicated KABC radio-talk show. His most recent books are *The Unreality Industry* (1989, with W. Bennis), *We're So Big and Powerful That Nothing Bad Can Happen to Us* (1990, with T. C. Pauchant), *Transforming the Crisis-Prone Organization* (1992, with T. C. Pauchant), and *The Unbounded Mind* (1993, with H. Linstone).

RICHARD O. MASON is Carr P. Collins Professor of Management Information Sciences at the Edwin L. Cox School of Business at Southern Methodist University. He received his B.S. degree (1956) from Oregon State University in business and technology and his Ph.D. degree (1968) from the University of California, Berkeley, in business administration.

Mason consults to numerous corporations, including General Motors, Hughes Aircraft, J. C. Penney, Kodak, the U.S. Census Bureau, the U.S. Forest Service, Wells Fargo Bank, and Xerox. He is a member of the board of the Hopi Foundation and serves in an advisory capacity to Parkland Hospital, the City of Dallas, and the AAA's "Project 2061—Education for a Changing Future" in San Antonio, Texas.

Mason's current areas of research include strategy and information systems, the history of information systems, and social and ethical implications of information systems. He recently completed a three-year term on the GMAC Commission to examine the future role of graduate management education and was selected in 1989 to be a delegate to the USSR to review Soviet plans for the "Informatization of Soviet Society." In 1992, Mason was elected as a foreign member of the Russian Academy of Natural Sciences in the "Information and Cybernetics" section.

Mason's academic publications have appeared in numerous business and management journals. His books include *Challenging Strategic Planning Assumptions* (1981, with I. I. Mitroff), *Strategic Management and Business Policy* (1982, with A. Rowe and K. Dickel), and *Managing with Style* (1987, with A. J. Rowe).

CHRISTINE M. PEARSON is former associate director of the Center for Crisis Management at the University of Southern California. She received her B.A. degree (1973) from Queens College of the City University of New York in French and economics, her M.S. degree (1983) from California State University, Long Beach, in industrial psychology, and her Ph.D. degree (1988) from the University of Southern California in business.

Pearson's research focuses on the impact of organizational culture on crisis management and the human contribution to the cause and escalation of organizational crises, particularly in the petrochemical and service industries. She has published articles on these topics in *Industrial Crisis Quarterly*, *Academy of Management Executive*, and *Organization Science*.

As a consultant, Pearson has assisted in the implementation of long-term, system-wide change for a variety of public and private organizations, including American

Honda, Chevron, First Interstate Bank, Red Cross, and the State of California. Much of the framework introduced in this book is based on her research collaboration with line workers, managers, and executives of Clorox, Dow Chemical, Kraft-General Foods, Mobil Oil, Occidental Petroleum, Taco Bell, and Transamerica Life Corporation.

FRAMEBREAK

PART ONE

BUSINESS

NOT AS

USUAL

ONE

THE DEMISE
OF THE MODERN
ORGANIZATION

These are hard times for business. The large bureaucracies of the nineteenth and twentieth century have become victims of their past success. They are trapped inside a form that no longer works. "Large corporations like GM often stubbornly resist change, as underscored by the crisis now gripping such American giants as IBM, Sears, and Citicorp. . . . Their size usually helps them forestall change for too long, so that when the forces finally become irresistible, the upheaval resembles the centrifugal breakup of the Soviet Union," proclaimed *Time* magazine in late 1992.[1]

But "centrifugal breakup" isn't the inevitable ending to the story of organizational obsolescence. Companies that acknowledge and even embrace the need for change are demonstrating that there are alternatives. Some organizations have begun experimenting with radical new designs in response to the challenges they are facing. Consider the example of Xerox.

American Samurai

Xerox dominated the copier business since its inception in 1959. During the 1970s, however, Xerox began to lose market share to Japanese companies such as Canon, Sharp, Minolta, Ricoh, and Matsushita (maker of Panasonic). From 1976 to 1982, Xerox's worldwide share of copier revenues dropped from 82 percent to 41 percent. Xerox had assumed it could sell anything it made simply by exercising its considerable sales and market power, but by late 1980 it had become clear that its Japanese competitors had wrenched away much of that power. Former CEO and chairman C. Peter McColough recalls, "We were horrified to find that the Japanese were selling their small machines for what it cost us to make ours. Our costs were not only way out in left field, they weren't even in the ballpark. Let me tell you, that was scary, and it woke us up in a hurry."[2]

McColough and his successor David Kearns, the company's leading executives at the time, began the painful process of organizational transformation. In 1981, a massive job cutting program was undertaken, while at the same time efforts were initiated to cut the number of suppliers. Eventually, Xerox's list of qualified suppliers was reduced from more than five thousand to fewer than five hundred. More importantly, the company developed a new product line—the Series 10—and introduced it in 1982. It was backed by a new management philosophy that was founded on several key concepts: an emphasis on quality, competitive benchmarking, pushing responsibility down in the organization, a sharper focus on the customer, more emphasis on market research, total globalization of the business, faster business processes, just-in-time manufacturing, automation and computerization, and—using the Series 10 as a rallying point—a commitment to stay on the leading edge of technology, thereby making it difficult for the Japanese to take advantage of their automated plants.

The turnaround began to take hold in 1983. That year, Xerox increased its market share by about two or three points, becoming the first major American manufacturer to regain market share from the Japanese and thereby earning the nickname American Samurai. The company's U.S. copier market share reached 10 percent in 1985 and continued to rise steadily.

When Paul Allaire became CEO in 1990, he dedicated himself to taking the company's corporate transformation to an even higher level. Allaire's Xerox is driven by a new vision of how it can serve people: Xerox—the document company. It has carved out as its special niche those areas of information processing where paper is converted to electronics and information is converted to paper: "We believe that documents—whether in electronic or paper form—are the key to making organizations more efficient," Allaire observes. "By focusing on managing documents and using them more effectively, Xerox can help our customers improve productivity."[3]

The new corporate vision has demanded additional organizational changes. In the new organizational architecture, as Allaire likes to call it, Xerox's divisions resemble independent businesses and incorporate nearly all of the classical management functions. Three separate geographical units sell and service all Xerox machines. Staff has been reduced. Layers of management have been cut out. Line managers have been given more authority and responsibility. Specialized workers, who formerly were organized into clusters, are now assigned to specific projects. For example, engineers are now working with marketing specialists to build copiers that satisfy customer needs. Workers are allowed to respond directly to the marketplace and required to make more decisions to save time and money.

The roles of president and CEO have been replaced by a six-person corporate office headed by Allaire himself. The corporate office operates in a bottom-up fashion. In the past, the business's priorities were set at the top and communicated downward as part of the planning process. In the new organization, the process is completely reversed. Business leaders develop their own priorities and communicate them up to the corporate office.

Allaire believes that three factors make all of this work. Among them are formal business processes, which he refers to as "hardware" and which include the company's basic technology core. Another factor is people. People need not only the skills but also the personality, attitudes, and overall health to operate effectively in the new environment. The third factor embraces the corporate culture, its value system, and the informal networks and practices linking people together. Allaire calls this the "software" and is dedicated to developing it to fit the new business climate.

Carrying out all of these changes requires considerable fortitude. "It's gut wrenching," Allaire observes. But these initiatives have helped Xerox become an 18-billion-dollar company and regain an 18 percent market share. Its 1991 earnings were $454 million, up 87 percent from 1990.

As this example illustrates, the demise of the modern organization doesn't necessarily mean its downfall. If management embraces the opportunity for a radical reconceptualization, the modern organization can be transformed and made far more functional. Either way, the fact remains that the modern organization must change. Organizations simply cannot be designed, operated, or managed as they have been in the past.

M-Form Dysfunction

In spite of all the talk and writing in recent years about the need for fundamental restructuring and change if America's organizations are to be competitive in global markets, most organizations are still vestiges of an outworn nineteenth- and early twentieth-century model pioneered by companies like General Motors, DuPont, Standard Oil, and Sears. These organizations were multifunctional, multidivisional, and hierarchical. This model, as the noted business historian Alfred Chandler observes, was enormously successful for managing the expansion of industrial capitalism.[4] As a result, the superiority of the multidivisional, or *M-form*, organization soon became clear, and most other companies followed suit.[5]

Since 1945, organizations have largely followed three major principles in the design and operation of their businesses:

1. Put separate business functions such as accounting, law, and marketing into separate, autonomous departments.

2. Put different products into separate product lines.

3. Put separate geographical regions into separate business units.

In one way or another, these principles not only undergirded the M-form organization but also led to its becoming the most prevalent type today. The M-form provided a way to deal effectively with the huge costs and problems involved in inventing and operating the large manufacturing systems that were required to develop and service mass markets.

However, the M-form has outlived its usefulness. It now creates more problems than it solves. Why? Because M-form organizations cannot meet the challenges of today's fast-paced, dynamically changing, information-intensive, globalized business environment.

The M-form permitted economies of scale by breaking down, compartmentalizing, and standardizing virtually all key business functions and operations. But this means that the M-form is rigid and inflexible in the face of rapid change. It is unable to cope with the myriad of interactions and interconnections that characterize modern business conditions and problems. In today's world, complex business problems require solutions that cut simultaneously across functions like accounting, finance, production, and law; across different product lines; and across geographical regions.

Consider, for instance, the challenge posed by our planet's environmental problems. This challenge demands that we view an organization as a whole system so that we can assess how its manufacturing processes and operations constitute and produce threats to the environment. We cannot, in other words, view the parts of an organization in isolation. Yet this is precisely what some of the older, traditional business functions such as accounting and law instruct us to do. In today's world, we cannot separate the "legal" aspects of pollution from the "political" or "strategic" ones—or any others for that matter.

In addition, the hallmarks of the M-form organization— mass production, mass marketing, and mass distribution— no longer correspond to the realities of the marketplace. Product life cycles have been shortened considerably by constant innovation. Indeed, new products are often obsolete before they are even introduced. Economic lot sizes are also considerably smaller. With modern computer- and communication-based technologies, it is possible to make small runs of increasingly customized goods and services and to deliver them to highly specialized markets. All of these activities can take place anywhere in the world, since they are coordinated by global information networks that operate twenty-four hours a day. Many business and manufacturing activities are being *outsourced*—that is, conducted by contractors, agents, partners, subsidiaries, and the like that are not permanent parts of organizations themselves. Former internal divisions and functions are dispersed throughout the world and are changed with respect to the pace, scope, and content of their activities.

All of this adds up to a radical change in the environment of business. The conditions for which the M-form organization was designed, and in which it thrived, have changed so drastically that the old design is incapable of meeting today's problems.

Business Not as Usual

To summarize, M-form organizations are in trouble because their operating assumptions are outmoded. Their most basic and taken-for-granted assumption is that *an organization is a machine*. To this way of thinking, an organization is made up of separate, freestanding, autonomous departments, functions, and objectives. A further assumption is that each of the basic functions, such as accounting, finance, law, marketing, manufacturing, and planning, are independent of one another and thus need only be integrated at the top. In addition, new programs or functions can be added indefinitely without changing the basic structure, functions, or purposes of the organization.

Realizing that business cannot continue as usual, many M-form organizations have launched well-intentioned initiatives that have only served to complicate the problem. Executives have proposed and implemented a bewildering variety of new programs and have tried to overlay them on existing organizational structures. But no organization can effectively conduct its regular business while also trying to incorporate the latest management craze or fad into its operations. In times of stringent economic conditions in which downsizing and cost cutting are the norm, the agendas of most organizations are already full. They do not have the resources to perform their primary businesses well, let alone take on new or ancillary functions. As a result, new programs have become additional sources of alienation and confusion for employees, who become burned out, depressed, cynical, and even suicidal.

The alternative to patching up a faulty structure built on outmoded assumptions is to take a long step back and reconceptualize the organization as a whole. That's what the management of Xerox began to do, and other companies as well have faced the need for change and begun moving in the right direction. A couple of brief examples will serve to illustrate some of the other radical solutions currently being tried.

Semco is a diversified manufacturing company in Brazil that in 1988 had a profit margin of 10 percent on sales of $37 million. A short time before, it was on the verge of collapse. As a result, its leadership inaugurated a new way of doing business that challenged and reversed many accepted principles of management. It began to treat its employees like adults. It eliminated time clocks, dress codes, and rules and regulations. It placed its employees in the "demanding position of using their own judgment," involving them, through company-wide voting, in most important corporate decisions and giving them access to the company's financial records and plans.[6] It instituted job rotation, profit sharing, and work groups that appoint their own leaders. It reorganized itself so that no business unit was larger than 150 people, and there were no more than three layers of management, thus rejecting the typical pyramidal structure of most organizations. Periodically, Semco's employees are asked what it would take for them to strike or quit, so that management can better understand the company's weaknesses. The result of all these radical changes has been that Semco has staged a strong comeback.

Chaparral Steel, a U.S. corporation, resolved to become the world's low-cost producer of steel. Its CEO, Gordon Forward, focused on three ideas: a classless corporation, universal education, and freedom to act.[7] In Chaparral's classless organization, workers set their own hours and can park next to the CEO but are expected to take the initiative in their work and use their heads to get the job done. At least 85 percent of Chaparral's 950 employees are enrolled in courses at any one time. This investment in people pays off in lower costs, as when Chaparral was designing a new mill for making wide-flanged steel beams. The employees developed technology that reduces the number of times the product passes through the manufacturing system from fifty to twelve or fewer.

As Xerox, Semco, and Chaparral Steel show, dramatic experiments *are* taking place. Organizations *are* innovating. Radically new designs for the twenty-first century *are* emerging.

Still, these three organizations are rare exceptions, not the norm. And although they are moving in the right direction, our contention nonetheless is that their experiments have not gone far or deep enough and have not encompassed all the dimensions of the change that is needed.

What is needed—and what we are proposing in this book—is nothing less than a concerted experiment based on a new theory of business that sees organizations as complex systems and transforms every dimension of how business is currently done.

Survival requires that this radical reconceptualization be undertaken. There is, in fact, no alternative. Those organizations that take change seriously will survive; those that do not will cease to exist.

TWO

A VISION
OF THE NEW
ORGANIZATION

Radical new designs for business are called for. In the preceding chapter, we discussed the reasons why and gave examples of some of the bold initiatives being taken by organizations. In this chapter, we take a closer look at the complex problems facing business today and suggest the broad outlines of a new organizational form designed to cope with them.

As one example of a business in which the environment has grown steadily more complex, consider the fast-food industry.

The Parable of the Hamburger

Selling hamburgers used to be a nice, simple business.

Barely forty years ago, a proprietor owned a single hamburger stand—or two or three at most, in the same city.

Chances were good that the owner-manager grew up with his or her employees, suppliers, and customers. As a result, he or she could count on their loyalty and trustworthiness.

Best of all, selling hamburgers was an easy business to get into. It didn't require the half million dollars and up needed today to open a major national fast-food franchise. A local niche was easily established by virtue of a special location, a distinctive name, the crowd served, the architectural design, the mood projected, the type of music or style of dress featured, and perhaps a secret recipe.

Today, everything is different.

First, and perhaps most important, a fast-food restaurant is likely to be part of a nationwide chain of some two thousand or so outlets. As a consequence, a sizable chunk of up-front cash is needed to launch the business. In return, the franchisee gets all the benefits, as well as all the headaches, of being part of a large organization.

What is served, as well as how it is prepared, is dictated by the main headquarters of the franchise. Headquarters also determines and funds major marketing campaigns and promotions, which might include the distribution of special premiums, toys, and gadgets.

In exchange for these so-called benefits, each outlet returns a proportion of its profits to headquarters. The profits fund the corporate structure and such functions as public relations, quality assurance, corporate and field security, and district management of the outlets.

For every benefit there is a corresponding cost. Anything that threatens corporate headquarters threatens each of the field outlets as well, and vice versa. In 1991, for example, McDonald's was sued for $10 million by the family of a six-year-old who was injured on a merry-go-round at a McDonald's playground.[1] The safety of the playgrounds at all McDonald's outlets was called into question as a result. Likewise, the mere rumor of product tampering or food alteration can cause a nationwide crisis. Such was the case when McDonald's was falsely accused of putting worms in its products to lower costs.

There are many questions that have to be asked when a franchisee is part of a large national and international chain. For instance, are the food packaging materials provided by headquarters biodegradable? Do they pose a perceived threat to the environment so that local environmental groups may boycott the outlet? Does headquarters secure its beef at the expense of the environment—for instance, from the rain forests of South America? Though national attention may not fall upon the corporation, the local outlet may still receive protests. Given the recent changes in diet and the growing concern with health, are the chain's products associated with poor nutrition?

If a franchisee opens an outlet in a foreign capital, is continued access to supplies guaranteed? For instance, in the case of the new Soviet Republics, one literally has to ship in all of one's beef, since everything is in short supply there. Or consider another prominent issue: A virtue of being associated with a large food chain is consistency of products and atmosphere. Thus, no matter where a consumer may be, he or she will always be able to experience the comfort of the familiar. And consistency is comforting for many consumers. But how does one maintain and ensure the consistency of products from neighborhood to neighborhood, city to city, state to state, and even country to country? This issue involves not only setting basic standards in the first place, but also ensuring that the standards will be met.

A critical issue that affects every business is the effect of lower educational standards and the absence of a trained work force. If employees cannot read, or the level of reading skills continues to drop precipitously, what alternatives are available? One solution in the fast-food business is to place pictures of menu items directly on cash register buttons so that an illiterate work force can serve the public. Many fast-food outlets, such as the Mrs. Fields cookie stores, are run with the aid of a computer-based management system that greatly reduces the need for educated, literate personnel.

Increasing longevity precipitates another issue. As the work force continues to age, is a company hiring older employees, who presumably have better educational skills? Further, as older workers grow in number, can they force the passage of antidiscrimination laws that will affect all companies?

Other serious issues arise. One of the locations in which fast-food businesses do well is the inner city. But this is precisely the area in which some of the most serious ills of urban America are to be found. What happens if an outlet becomes identified with certain gangs? What happens if rival gangs adopt different locations? What hazards are imposed on innocent bystanders?

Or consider the issue of corporate ethics. When

McDonald's sponsored "Ronald McDonald's Family The-
ater" on CBS, the Center for the Study of Commercialism
in Washington, D.C., objected that the presence of Ronald
McDonald as host was the equivalent of a commercial.[2] Is
it ethical to commercialize children's TV programming in
such a way?

None of these issues faced the owner of a hamburger
stand forty years ago. In those days, simple organizations
sufficed because business problems were relatively simple.
A proprietor sold hamburgers and nothing else. A proprietor operated a hamburger stand, not playgrounds.

The primary difference is this: in a simple world, problems are bounded (one sells hamburgers, not toys or anything else); problems stay put (they don't change or expand—they don't involve the rain forests of Brazil); they
can thus be compartmentalized (the finance department
handles the financial aspects of the business and nothing
else; the legal department, the liabilities; and so on).
However, in a complex world, there are no simple,
bounded problems. Problems continually expand and spill
over to involve every aspect of the business.

A Total Systems Approach

In the previous chapter we mentioned the assumptions underlying the old M-form organization. Because of the
changed realities of our complex world, a whole new set
of assumptions is more appropriate for our time. The most
basic assumption is that *all organizations are complex*

systems that interact constantly and significantly with a host of other equally complex systems. The most important property of these systems is that they cannot be broken down into parts that have separate lives of their own. Thus, in an organization, no basic functions, departments, or objectives exist independently of one another. Everything not only interacts with everything else but is an intrinsic part of everything else as well. A corollary is that one obtains a highly distorted and seriously misleading picture of any part of a system if one attempts to study and manage it apart from the larger system in which it exists.

Given the complex interrelationships that characterize business today, the basic functions of organizations are changing radically. All of the new corporate functions that we currently see emerging—signified by new positions like chief information officer; director of health, safety, and environmental affairs; director of ethics programs; head of crisis management; director of issues management; vice president for total quality management; chief officer of globalism—address systematic problems that cut across the traditional areas of accounting, finance, law, marketing, human resources, and strategic planning. These new functions not only address systemic problems but also interrelate among themselves. Each has implications for all the others. Clearly, a new organizational structure is required to accommodate these new functions.

We have identified six new interrelated functions that we believe are critical for organizations to incorporate in some way alongside the traditional functions. We have also identified four key dimensions of a new organizational structure designed to support the critical functions. We'll look closely at the new functions and their interrelationships in this chapter and will briefly outline the four key organizational dimensions. The remainder of the book is devoted to detailing those four dimensions and envisioning the organization of which they will be a part.

Six New Key Functions of Business

The six new functions we've identified as critical for meeting today's challenges are issues management, crisis management, total quality management, environmentalism, globalism, and ethics. Businesses must be competent in these areas if they expect to compete globally. Two basic activities are vital to the development of the new functions: (1) a series of audits or assessments to determine an organization's strengths and weaknesses with respect to each function, and (2) a series of designs and/or redesigns of the basic structure of an organization so that it can carry out each new function.

Issues Management. Recall from our hamburger-chain example that everything affecting a particular hamburger franchisee is also potentially affecting headquarters, and vice versa. As a result, it has become a critical priority to sense and track long-term societal trends (for example, the change in dietary habits or the decline in the literacy of the work force) *before* they become problems or major crises for a particular hamburger outlet or for a fast-food corporation as a whole. Issues management is the function responsible for performing this critical assessment. Ideally, the tracking of such trends should be part of strategic planning. In recent years, however, many companies have cut back their strategic planning departments or restricted their scope to short-term financial planning. In addition, the changes that are occurring are often too rapid and abrupt for strategic planning departments to handle.

Besides tracking broad societal and industry-wide trends, issues management focuses on determining and assessing issues that pose a specific threat or opportunity and identifying the stakeholders associated with those issues; assessing the power of the opposition versus the company in shaping issues; and determining how opposing stakeholders and associated issues will affect the products, services, manufacturing processes, and reputation of the company.[3] In short, issues management is concerned primarily with sensing and tracking important trends and general issues in the *external environment* of organizations that can cause or force significant *internal changes* in the way organizations are designed and operated.

Crisis Management. Crisis management, on the other hand, is concerned primarily with major internal and external forces that can threaten the existence of an entire organization. An employee, or even a nationwide network of employees, may set out to poison hamburgers, for example, thus damaging the firm's reputation. External saboteurs can also threaten an organization, perhaps by circumventing corporate security to poison the firm's food products.

At the core of crisis management is a series of ongoing, interrelated assessments or audits of the kinds of crises and forces that threaten the main products, services, manufacturing processes, employees, and surrounding environment of a company. Crisis management encompasses the design and implementation of plans, procedures, and mechanisms for the detection of, possible prevention of, preparation for, containment of, and recovery and learning from key crises.[4]

Total Quality Management. Total quality management (TQM) is concerned with the design and use of proper equipment and processes to produce the highest-quality products and services. One of the key objectives of total quality management is to assess the sources of defects in the manufacturing and management systems of an organization. The literature on total quality management constantly stresses that product defects are typically due not to careless individual operators but rather to the tools operators have been given, the failure of management to design and implement effective production processes, and the presence of beliefs that management may be more interested in getting products out the door than in ensuring their quality.[5] Defects or poor quality may also be due to poor initial designs, raw materials, and shipping and distribution systems. Total quality management seeks the redesign of products, processes, and systems when necessary and aims for continuous improvement in all phases of company operations.

Environmentalism. Environmentalism is concerned primarily with assessing the threats that products and the manufacturing and distribution processes pose to the environment and local communities. Environmentalism is also concerned with the design or redesign of products and manufacturing processes to make them beneficial to the environment. For instance, the containers in which fast-food hamburgers are packaged used to be made of styrofoam, but objections from environmentalists have resulted in the design of recyclable paper boxes that meet requirements for heat retention, cleanliness, and aesthetics.

Attention to environmental concerns can actually create profit-making opportunities. For example, Gail Mayville, an office manager at Ben and Jerry's, the Vermont ice-cream maker, noted that the company wasn't being as proactive as it might be in managing solid waste and conserving resources.

> So Mayville took the initiative, beginning with the company's chronic sewage problem. She fed the sludge left over from the manufacture of ice cream to pigs, and she poured the remainder on farm land as fertilizer, for a profit. Then she recycled the ten bales of cardboard the company was dumping each week and saved $17,500 per year. After that, she found a way—one that others had deemed technically impossible—to recycle the fifty thousand four-and-a-half gallon plastic buckets the company uses to hold ice-cream ingredients, and she saved 78 percent of the cost of dumping. And on

and on she went, using entrepreneurial imagination to turn social costs into company savings and profits.[6]

Globalism. Globalism reflects the reality that national and regional economies are now inextricably linked together. Among the global concerns of business is the identification of new worldwide markets for its products. Globalism is also concerned with assessing the international marketability of products and with adapting and modifying them to meet local needs around the globe.

Globalism requires that an organization's production, marketing, and administrative processes be tuned to the global political economy. On the marketing side, it involves the identification and development of new products and markets, country by country, to serve different cultural needs and preferences. It also involves adapting products and procedures to meet local requirements. On the production side, globalism requires a full look at all locations throughout the world in which supplies may be procured and business activities conducted. Globalism challenges executives to find the best "global division of labor."

Ethics. Every organization faces ethical questions having to do with its key business principles and how they affect the health and safety of employees, consumers, and the environment. A viable ethics program examines the ethical and moral attributes of the organization's behavior, policies, decisions, and procedures and assesses their contribution to the realization of a good and just community.

It designs (or redesigns), explains, and implements controls, codes, and credos to ensure that the ethics of the organization are known and upheld.

How the Six Functions Interrelate

The six new functions we've just described are fundamentally related, and none can be carried out effectively without the others. The problem of instilling, say, total quality management in an organization is inseparable from the problem of instilling environmentalism or crisis management. For instance, if an organization ignores how its manufacturing, operating, and distribution processes pose threats to the environment, it may cause a crisis down the line. If done properly, issues management can sense potential environmental problems before they become major crises for an organization. And, conversely, catching potential internal crises early enough can prevent possible threats to the environment.

Consider this assessment of the overlap between environmentalism and total quality management:

> In industries as diverse as consumer products, chemicals, and electronics, environmental performance has become a new frontier for quality management. And with good reason. U.S. companies spend more than $60 billion a year to comply with environmental laws, and the costs will soar as the 1990 Clean Air Act takes hold. By linking quality to

environmental goals, companies from Xerox and Procter and Gamble to Allied-Signal and IBM have found that they can cut pollution and improve compliance, often while lowering their environmental costs. And quality management can "become a road map to pollution prevention, which puts you ahead of regulations."[7]

Consider some other interrelationships. Total quality management can lead to the creation of new products that can open up new global markets, while globalism can feed relevant information back that shows the need for greater quality in the manufacturing of new or existing products. Ethics is closely linked to crisis management because it acknowledges the sources of organizational malfunction and dysfunction that can create a crisis. It is also linked to total quality management, because quality, in its deepest sense, involves the creation of a good and just society by means of business products, services, and deeds.

Each function is both a *contributor* to and a *beneficiary* of the other functions. Table 2.1 shows these interrelationships. Read across the table to see what each of the functions contributes to the others; read down the table to see what each of the functions receives from the others. It is essential to manage these six functions according to how they interrelate.

The same holds true for the traditional functions of business, which are no longer more important than the new functions. Every function must be seen as a fundamental part of all the others, as providing critical knowl-

TABLE 2.1. Interrelationships Among the Functions.

Beneficiaries

	Crisis Management	Issues Management	Total Quality Management
Crisis Management		Identifies vulnerabilities that can turn into major negative issues; leads to preparedness	Identifies and eliminates potential manufacturing defects
Issues Management	Identifies potential issues that can turn into major crises		Identifies potential threats to quality and/or demands for quality
Total Quality Management	Identifies and eliminates potential product-related crises	Eliminates potential issues	
Environ-mentalism	Identifies and eliminates potential industrial disasters	Identifies and eliminates potential environmental issues	Identifies potential threats and challenges to quality
Globalism	Identifies potential international crises	Identifies potential international issues	Identifies international quality standards and new products
Ethics	Identifies sources of ethics-related crises	Identifies values and community issues	Helps specify quality

Contributors

Beneficiaries

Environmen-talism	Globalism	Ethics
Identifies and eliminates potential environmental threats	Identifies potential competitive weaknesses in the global arena	Leads to awareness of vulnerabilities to ethical lapses
Identifies potential environmental issues and threats	Identifies new markets and losses of markets	Gives early warning of upcoming ethics problems
Eliminates potential environmental threats and issues	Improves product competitiveness	Leads to awareness of product liabilities and employee satisfaction
	Identifies new markets for new products	Identifies external stakeholders
Identifies new markets for environmentally beneficial products		Identifies value differences among peoples
Values nature and the land	Addresses worldwide value issues	

edge related to key concerns. For example, consider the fields of accounting, finance, marketing, and environmentalism. New relationships are developing that promise to revolutionize each of them. Accounting and environmentalism are coming together to form the new field of environmental accounting, which is concerned with developing new methods of measuring the "true and total" assets and liabilities of a firm with regard to its products and resulting waste materials. Environmental accounting thus aims to promote new products and services, along with manufacturing and distribution processes, that benefit the environment. The same is happening with environmentalism and finance, or *green finance*, and environmentalism and marketing, or *green marketing*. In the case of green marketing, the intent is to develop new ways of selling environmentally sound products and services and to expand the market for such products and services.

In addition to being interrelated, the six new functions are systemic. A project conducted by the University of Southern California Center for Crisis Management found that those organizations with the most effective environmentalism programs have a systemic infrastructure for environmentalism that is similar to an effective structure for crisis management. These programs have a company-wide inventory of all the separate projects that are being conducted with regard to the environment. This enables various divisions of the organization to know what the others are doing so that they are not proceeding at cross purposes. In addition, there is a company-wide information system, a dedicated budget for environmentalism, and a senior officer who not only oversees environmentalism but also serves as its champion and representative at the highest levels of the organization. Lines of communication are open not only internally, so that all employees can understand company policy and participate in it, but also to external environmental groups, often those with which a company does not particularly agree. Finally, environmentalism is a fundamental part of every employee's job, becoming linked with each employee's "personal bottom line."

Serious programs built around the other five critical functions also require a system-wide company effort. For instance, thinking globally has to be as much a part of every employee's job as quality and service. In a nutshell, *each of the six critical functions must be a part of every employee's job*. The fact that they are all systemic is precisely what distinguishes them from the more traditional functions.

An example will illustrate how the six functions might be managed as part of an integrated whole. To bring Lone Star Steel, one of two leading manufacturers of steel tubular goods, out of Chapter 11 during the time that their U.S. market was shrinking, CEO Rhye Best devised a global strategy in order to secure business in places like the North Sea and Indonesia (where oil field use of casings and tubing was growing). Lone Star's global strategy required an increased emphasis on quality in order to compete successfully with Japanese and German suppliers. But Best and his fellow executives soon learned that many of Lone Star's employees could not read and, hence, could not use the statistical quality control charts that are so vital to a successful program of total quality management. So the company became involved in providing literacy programs within both the plant and the community.

To compete with the Japanese, they had to reduce production cycles from 120 days to fewer than 34 days. This had to be accomplished without any reduction in the safety and health programs that had been put in place to avoid crises. Furthermore, all of this had to be achieved by means of technologies, methods, and procedures that met or exceeded current and anticipated U.S. environmental requirements, which, of course, are among the most stringent in the world. In effect, Lone Star managed each of the functions in Table 2.1 in conjunction with the others. In this way, they ensured that no function would be at odds with another and, further, that each function would build on the others.

New Functions, New Form

One of the basic assumptions of a total systems approach to organizations is that new programs cannot be added at will without changing profoundly the basic structure, functions, and purposes of organizations; no program, no matter how worthy or valuable, can be effective unless the larger system of which it is a part is also effective. Therefore, if the six new functions we have described are to be integrated and managed together, a new organizational structure is necessary. We envision a radical new structure that encompasses four major dimensions: (1) knowledge and learning, (2) recovery and development, (3) world service and spirituality, and (4) world-class operations.

1. *Knowledge and learning.* Information and knowledge are the lifeblood of organizations in today's world. Accurate information and knowledge are required in order to produce quality products that can compete worldwide without causing harm to people or the environment. As a result, every organization needs a means to gather, organize, and disseminate the right information to the right people at the right time so that the right products and services can be produced and delivered.

2. *Recovery and development.* Unhealthy organizations and employees cannot produce quality products or deliver quality services. Organizations affect the emotional well-being of employees more deeply and extensively than we have thus far recognized. Consequently, organizations need a means to identify and treat the dysfunctional processes at work.

3. *World service and spirituality.* Human beings do not leave their spiritual impulses at home when they come to work. These concerns need to find expression in some form of service to the world. Organizations must recognize these needs and channel them so that they contribute to the solution of world problems, such as hunger, homelessness, child abuse, and pollution. To put it somewhat differently, organizations have an obligation to promote well-being not only in their employees but in the world as well.

4. *World-class operations*. To be a major competitor in any industry requires constant innovation, research, and development. It entails close critical scrutiny of products, services, processes, and distribution strategies. Organizations need a means to carry on this scrutiny and incorporate the latest scientific and engineering knowledge pertaining to the design, manufacture, and operation of their products and services.

We argue that these four major concerns or dimensions—knowledge, health, service, and world-class operations—cannot be separated. They form an interlocking whole. Remove any one of them and an organization falters. Furthermore, the role of an organization's leadership is to tie together, integrate, and manage (not necessarily eliminate) the creative conflicts and tensions among the four concerns. These ideas are embodied in Figure 2.1.

These four dimensions have an impact on each of the main functions of an organization. None of the functions, whether new or traditional, can be performed effectively without (1) appropriate information and knowledge, (2) appropriate psychological treatment leading to healthy employees and a healthy company, (3) a sense of meaning and purpose gained from contributing to a healthy world environment, and (4) world-class manufacturing tools and operations.

Another way to look at how the four dimensions cut across and bolster the six new functions is to consider the various "voices" that need to be heard for an organization to succeed. Total quality management requires that cus-

FIGURE 2.1. The Four Dimensions of a New
Organizational Structure.

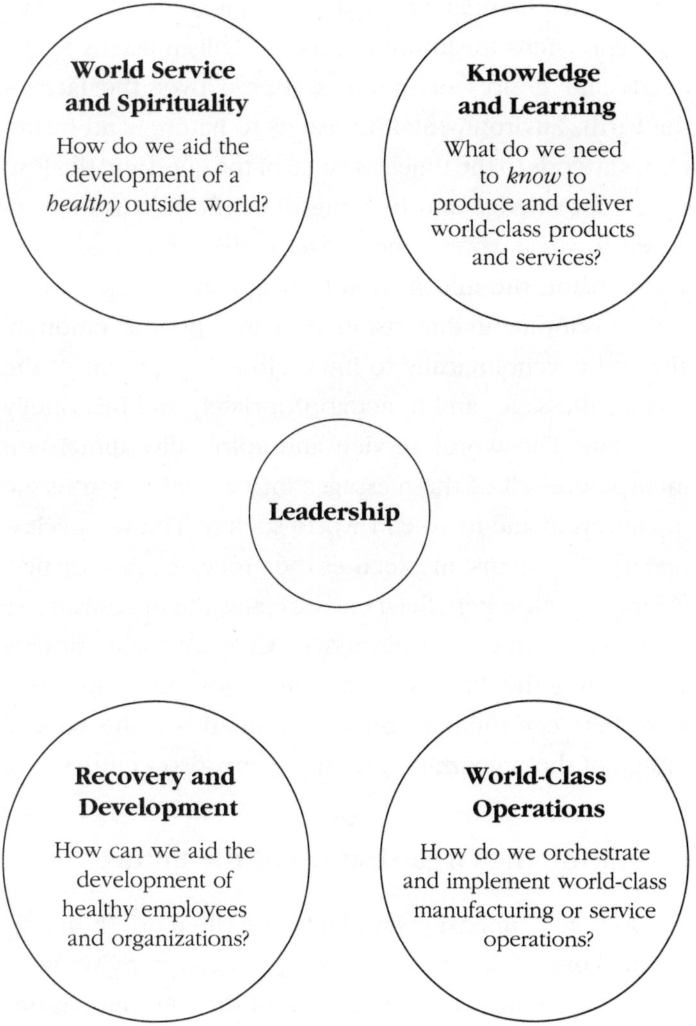

**World Service
and Spirituality**

How do we aid the
development of a
healthy outside world?

**Knowledge
and Learning**

What do we need
to *know* to
produce and deliver
world-class products
and services?

Leadership

**Recovery and
Development**

How can we aid the
development of
healthy employees
and organizations?

**World-Class
Operations**

How do we orchestrate
and implement world-class
manufacturing or service
operations?

35

tomers—with their unique desires and needs—be fully heard. Crisis management must listen to the voices of complexity, signalling the potential breakdown of complex systems or the potential for denying complexities. Issues management listens for future events. Globalism listens to the needs and desires of others scattered over the face of the earth. Environmentalism listens to nature. And finally, ethics attends to the timeless voice of the good and the just.

The knowledge and learning dimensions must stay attuned to these voices and sense, collect, process, store, and transmit the information they contain. The recovery and development dimension prepares people emotionally and psychologically to internalize the content of the various messages and to act appropriately and healthfully on them. The world service and spirituality dimension incorporates all of the messages into a total vision of the organization and its role in world society. The world-class operations dimension executes the processes that are necessary to realize beneficial ends. Finally, the organization's leadership, which we discuss in Chapter Eight, ties together all of the dimensions and manages the creative tensions between them. In broad outline, this is the skeletal design of the organization of the twenty-first century.

Designing the Organization of the Future

The four key dimensions we have described briefly are developed more fully in the following four chapters. We want to emphasize here that the notion of the four dimensions is not intended to add another layer of bureaucratic control. Ideally, the activities relating to each dimension need to be carried out at every level of an organization—for instance, through interlocking teams.[8] If a metaphor is needed, then that of a hologram is appropriate. The whole is in every part, and every part contains the whole.

We deliberately refrain from describing precisely the form these four key dimensions might take because ultimately it is the activities themselves that are vital, rather than their physical location or exact structure. There may well be an infinite number of designs incorporating the four dimensions, depending upon the particular organization and its businesses. If an organization embraces the concept of the total systems approach we describe, it will develop unique ways to embody the concept.

Our ideas are by no means utopian. Although no single organization currently embraces all of the dimensions and functions we describe, each of them is being applied on a limited basis by major organizations and government agencies.

The multinational Swiss pharmaceutical-chemical firm CIBA-GEIGY recently revamped its corporate vision and, to signify this, produced a new logo: a circle divided into three equal pie wedges, each wedge containing an icon reflecting a major aspect of CIBA-GEIGY's businesses or responsibilities. One wedge contains a chemical flask and a gear wheel, symbolic of CIBA-GEIGY's traditional business prowess and the fact that it must generate profits to survive. Another wedge contains a stylized outline of people, symbolic of the basic responsibility that CIBA-GEIGY holds toward its employees, their families, and the larger human community. The third wedge contains a representation of trees, symbolic of CIBA-GEIGY's responsibility toward the environment.

The company held a conference for its corporate communications officers from around the world to formulate strategies for communicating the new logo and underlying philosophy to its thousands of employees and external stakeholders. The president-CEO of the company was present to signal the importance of the effort. At a question-and-answer session, one member of the conference audience raised the point that well-developed measures to gauge economic and business performance already existed, but no such measures existed for the other two wedges of the new logo. The president-CEO replied, "Yes, I know. That's why we're going to have to develop these new measures together. Look! All of you are adults. You've asked for greater empowerment; I'm giving it to you! I'm asking both of us working together to develop new measures against which all of us will be evaluated."

We issue a similar challenge with this book. We need to guide our organizations to new knowledge, emotional health, spirituality, and global operations expertise. This is a daunting task, but human beings are endlessly creative. Given a guiding vision, we have proven time and again that we can rise to nearly any challenge.

PART TWO

THE

NEW ORDER

OF BUSINESS

THREE

KNOWLEDGE
AND LEARNING

In the previous chapter, we outlined a total systems approach to managing the organization of the twenty-first century. We emphasized the notions of inseparability and interconnectedness. In particular, we discussed how the new key functions of business and the new key dimensions of a supportive organizational structure interrelate.

Knowledge and information will perform a vital integrative role in the organization of the future. This dimension of an organization will concern itself with gathering, organizing, and disseminating the kinds of knowledge and information that are needed to perform the key management functions in an integrated and systemic manner. An essential part of this mission will be to keep track of critical business assumptions.

The Critical Importance of Assumptions

One of the major zoos in the United States was faced with a crisis: they were charged with abusing the elephants under their care.[1] Zoo administrators were concerned about how this charge would affect the zoo's reputation and, consequently, the community donations on which it depended. A few months after the crisis had simmered down, and after the zoo's reputation had been damaged, Mitroff was called in to help the top managers of the zoo see whether any critical lessons could be learned from their experience.

Working together, they did something that few managers and executives do: they determined what their belief system had been before the crisis and evaluated how the crisis had affected their beliefs.[2] Slowly but surely, about thirty major assumptions emerged. Every single assumption upon which they had been basing their behavior was proved invalid by the crisis.

The challenging of assumptions is a difficult exercise both intellectually and emotionally. People have to admit, to themselves and in front of others, that some of the things they have long believed about their organization, or themselves, are no longer true—if they ever were. In effect, they have to challenge some of their most fundamental beliefs about the world.

At the end of the day, thirty assumptions were summarized on a flipchart for all to see. It was readily apparent that they fell into three distinct clusters, each consisting of about ten assumptions each. An interesting portrait emerged that applied not only to this organization but to many others as well, especially those of a technical nature.

The first cluster of assumptions related to the credibility of the zoo. In one way or another, all ten assumptions in this group expressed the fact that this organization truly believed that its scientific standing gave credibility to whatever it said. If it said that it had not abused elephants, then the outside world would believe it. As these managers and executives learned painfully, the outside world is not composed of scientists. While it is absolutely necessary for the zoo to maintain its high scientific credibility and standing, this by itself is not enough to gain and retain the confidence of a general public that is often distrustful of scientists.

The second cluster of assumptions pertained to the belief that the zoo's employees would not sabotage or betray them. And yet it was employees who released to the press the allegations of animal abuse—by other employees.

The final cluster of assumptions related to the belief that if a crisis happened, the zoo's sister animal-care organizations would rush to its defense. In the past, the zoo had worked with diverse organizations on such issues as the protection of animals and thus assumed that in its hour of need, these organizations would close ranks and help it. How wrong they were.

If a major crisis has anything to teach us, it is this: a crisis does not challenge only one or two critical beliefs. Almost any organization can survive if one or two of its tenets are threatened. A crisis, almost by definition, threatens *every* belief. In fact, this is precisely what distinguishes a crisis from a minor incident or accident.

The moral of this story is that the kind of information and knowledge supplied by the traditional accounting, finance, and marketing functions is not sufficient to run complex organizations. Other kinds of information, such as an awareness of the business's critical assumptions, are equally important and must be kept track of systematically.

Integrative Knowledge

Ideas and knowledge are the lifeblood of today's organizations. The right information conveyed at the right time to the right people is what enables effective decision making in an organization. As a result, the gathering, organization, and dissemination of information cannot be left to chance, any more than contemporary organizations leave the collection of timely and accurate knowledge of their financial resources to chance. Indeed, virtually no one would propose that a major organization do without a permanent chief financial officer and a finance department. And yet many organizations still believe that it is not necessary to have a major unit that centralizes and integrates its knowledge and inquiry processes. Such a vital dimension cannot be left to chance.

In time, organizations will realize the importance of systemic management of the new business functions that we discussed in the last chapter. Issues management (the sensing of important external issues, such as ageism and feminism, that affect the operation and business of modern corporations), crisis management (the ability to prevent and to mitigate catastrophes before they happen), total quality management (the ability to produce quality products that can compete worldwide), environmentalism (the use of production and manufacturing processes that are environmentally sound, as well as products that are beneficial to the environment), ethics (the identification and honoring of values that an ethical organization should stand for and reflect in its processes and products), and globalism (the ability to sense and to develop new product markets worldwide) must be seen as one if they are to be managed successfully. Knowledge can perform an integrative role, illuminating the interrelationship of these functions.[3]

Critical functions, departments, and programs such as accounting, crisis management, environmentalism, finance, health and safety, human resources, issues management, law, marketing, strategic planning, and total quality management both produce and consume knowledge and information. Each provides special kinds of information and in turn makes use of other kinds of information from other parts of the organization. The ultimate goal is to deliver critical information to the decision makers who need it.

An essential but usually overlooked kind of integrative information is related to the taken-for-granted critical assumptions that affect every aspect of a business. Historically, identifying key assumptions was one of the jobs performed by strategic planning departments. However, strategic planning is often the captive of accounting and finance, thus diminishing the chances of developing a systemic view of the organization.

We are constantly amazed at how few organizations attempt even an inventory of their fundamental belief systems. We cannot claim with certainty that if General Motors regularly examined the critical assumptions upon which its businesses were founded, it would not be in the mess it is in today.[4] However, we would like to believe that if GM had instituted a process of identifying and challenging its most critical, sacred assumptions, it would have recognized the need to adapt to a changing world.

Consider another example. Recently, a major laundry company became involved with the Swedish car manufacturer Volvo.[5] In the beginning, the laundry's involvement was traditional, that is, restricted merely to cleaning the uniforms of Volvo's workers. As speedy as the laundry was in performing the service, Volvo wanted even quicker turnaround times. This led the laundry to request that it go inside Volvo's plants and inspect how the current uniforms were used. The result was that the laundry became involved not only in the redesign of the workers' uniforms but also in the manufacturing processes themselves. The outcome was a more efficient turnaround that benefited Volvo, its workers, and even the laundry service. This came about only because Volvo was willing to challenge the major assumption that customers, suppliers, or vendors do not need to become deeply involved in business operations. Once again, we see the fundamental role that assumptions play. Indeed, the examination and challenging of key assumptions is perhaps the most critical task facing every organization.

Envisioning the Knowledge and Learning Center

The knowledge and learning center of the organization of the future will collect, organize, and disseminate information while also acting as a systemic control mechanism. It will monitor how well programs and functions are achieving their own objectives as well as how much they are contributing to other programs and functions. The intent is *not* to add another bureaucratic mechanism, to exercise dictatorial control over every business function or unit of an organization, or to collect paralyzing mountains of data (which increasingly pass for knowledge in our civilization). Rather, it is to preserve the entrepreneurial freedom of the individual operating units while systematically informing the organization. The knowledge and learning center as we envision it has these major purposes:

- To collect, organize, centralize, and integrate information and knowledge from different parts of the organization to form a continually updated picture of the organization as a whole

- To measure and monitor how well each critical program and function is performing, achieving its objectives, and contributing to the success of other programs and functions

- To explore, examine, and probe the organization for critical linkages and synergy between key programs and functions and to ensure that they are exploited

- To identify, monitor, challenge, and replace critical assumptions that underlie key programs

- To insist and ensure that all important problems be examined from multiple perspectives so that the organization does not suffer from narrow vision

The knowledge and learning dimension, like the three other key dimensions of the organization of the future, will be recognized and institutionalized; it will have a permanent home and will be headed by an officer who will report directly to the CEO. We envision that this officer will receive a daily status report on the strengths and weaknesses of the company's programs and capabilities in crisis management, environmentalism, total quality management, global competitiveness or globalism, issues management, and ethics. She or he will also receive reports that summarize the strengths and weaknesses of the business's current products and services. The reports will integrate knowledge and information from accounting, finance, human relations, marketing, and strategic planning. The officer will also receive a daily report on the status of the company's twenty or so most critical business assumptions pertaining to every aspect of its operations. Much like the Dow Jones, the report will show the validity of each of the key assumptions of the past year relative to critical information. It will show which assumptions are especially in doubt and what the business impacts are likely to be if a particular assumption is no longer valid.

We must emphasize here that the exact form this dimension takes will vary from organization to organization. What is important is that its purposes be recognized and institutionalized in a way that is appropriate for the particular organization. As an example of what it might look like, we'll describe the case of the Learning/Inquiry Center at General Motors.

GM's Learning/Inquiry Center

GM's Learning/Inquiry Center is the brainchild of Vincent Barabba. Mitroff and Mason first met Barabba in 1974 when he served his first term as the director of the U.S. Bureau of the Census. At the time, Mitroff and Mason served as consultants on a project concerned with an idealized design of the bureau for the year 2000. During Barabba's second term, Mitroff and Mason served as policy consultants with regard to the conduct of the 1980 census.[6] At the end of his tenure as director of the census bureau, Barabba went on to serve as director of market intelligence at Xerox and Eastman Kodak. Mitroff and Mason worked with him as external consultants to help design information systems— or more broadly, *knowledge systems*—that would help both organizations gather effective knowledge that could be used to develop products that consumers needed and would buy. This was when we started developing our concept of the knowledge and learning dimension.

In his present job as executive in charge of the Market

Research Decision Center at General Motors, Barabba may have one of the most important marketing assignments in the United States. Because he was brought in from the outside and is not a product of GM's culture and internal career paths, Barabba has been able to develop GM's understanding of market processes and strategies along highly nontraditional, if not radical, lines. He has developed and implemented a new concept: the Learning/Inquiry Center. (The presence of the Learning/Inquiry Center indicates that GM's being in trouble does not necessarily mean that every one of its parts is. However, a troubled part is somewhat more likely to indicate a troubled whole. Either way, the health of the whole is not the same as the health of the parts.)

GM's Learning/Inquiry Center performs a number of critical functions. First and foremost, it is designed to tap into the voice of the market and to get that voice heard by the right people within GM so that cars can be produced that customers actually want. To accomplish this, Barabba and his staff have taken the company's first look at all of the elements of a marketing program from an integrated systems perspective. Thus, each program is judged not only on its own merits, standing by itself, but also with regard to how it contributes to the entire process necessary to gauge the market and transmit the information to the appropriate people.

In *Hearing the Voice of the Market*, Gerald Zaltman, professor of marketing at the Harvard Business School, and Barabba describe the Learning/Inquiry Center as they conceive of it. They explain that they use the term *inquiry center* to describe "the ideal state of mind within a company for effectively and efficiently reconciling the voice of the market with the voice of the firm." To them, the inquiry center is "a particular way of learning about the marketplace and using the resultant knowledge." Further, "while the term *center* describes an organizational unit, it is as much an attitude, ethic, or creed as it is a formal entity."

The fundamental purpose of the inquiry center is "to improve on and then institutionalize an ongoing process for drawing upon various sources of information, knowledge, data, and wisdom in order to bring them to bear on important decisions about the business (more than just vehicles)." Further purposes are "to build expertise and provide assistance to facilitate improved thinking, decisions, and actions, to break down the barriers between functions and foster/accelerate systemic thinking that is needed to produce quality, innovative products that are necessary in order to compete successfully in international markets," and "to increase the problem-setting and problem-solving capacity of managers by acquiring, synthesizing, developing, evaluating, and disseminating information." The center "challenges or makes managers aware of what they think they know, they think they need to know, they expect to happen given certain decisions, and assumptions they hold about the if-thens regarding decisions." Finally, the center "is a safe haven for exploring possibilities, dreams, visions, and fears."[7]

Zaltman and Barabba note that the center, rather than

simply gathering information about a specific problem, in some instances "might actually define and identify a potential problem before it becomes one."[8] Our notion of the knowledge and learning element builds on and extends the Learning/Inquiry Center notion of Zaltman and Barabba.

FOUR

RECOVERY AND DEVELOPMENT

If people and organizations were all brains and no feelings, then our discussion of the organization of the twenty-first century would have ended with the knowledge and learning element. But people and organizations are not thinking machines devoid of emotions; instead, they are exceedingly complex mixtures of thoughts and feelings. Thus, in addition to more and better knowledge and information, we require better ways of acknowledging and treating the emotional complexities, impediments, and dysfunctions of individuals and organizations.

Let us consider a real case that illustrates this need. While the names of the cities, companies, and individuals have all been disguised, the situation is not only real but all too common.

The Downfall of PubCore

Dave Markham and Robert Stewart came as a team to Midvail more than twenty-five years ago. They were lured away from a smaller company in the same business in another city. Midvail city leaders made them an offer "they couldn't refuse." Midvail wanted to move its company, PubCore, which was in the public service arena, into the "big leagues."

Dave and Bob, as CEO and COO, respectively, were given the mandate to build PubCore into a company with a national reputation. And build it they did. Under their leadership, PubCore not only grew in size but also won award after award for the quality of its products and services. Its name became virtually synonymous with excellence in the industry. It became a national and even an international model for success.

About four years ago, PubCore suffered a serious setback. It lost its major account. It was not only one that PubCore had had for years but also one that was very closely identified with PubCore in the public mind. The account—call it WorldVu—was an international household name.

WorldVu wanted to bring in house the services PubCore had provided for more than fifteen years and for which PubCore and WorldVu, acting together, had won every top award the public service industry had to offer. There were many reasons for the decision, most of which are not relevant here. WorldVu had hired an aggressive young executive who wanted to make a name for himself by showing he could do PubCore's job better and at less cost.

The separation was not only bitter but also lengthy—dragging on for more than two years. During this time, Dave and Bob were largely paralyzed because each had sunk into a depression as a result of losing WorldVu. PubCore suffered seriously as a consequence. Valuable time was lost during which Dave and Bob should have been planning and seeking new business.

In essence, Dave and Bob went through the same stages as those who have just learned that they have a terminal disease. First, they denied the situation altogether. They believed that WorldVu would somehow come to its senses and reverse its actions. When it finally became apparent that this was not going to happen, they then experienced anger. How could WorldVu treat them like this after all they had done for them and achieved together? Following denial and anger (although they never fully ceased), depression took over. This was the worst and longest-lasting emotional state of all.

Dave and Bob were, in effect, executives for good times. They had never really been forced to face a crisis. Not only were they stymied by the situation but, in many senses, they were devastated by it. They lost sleep, suffered anxiety, and generally became irritable and difficult to get along with. Saddest of all, they didn't seek professional help, even though it was apparent to many within PubCore that they needed it. Counseling, let alone psychotherapy, was completely out of the question. People from their "social class and background" didn't do "that kind of thing." Counseling and therapy were only for those who were seriously disturbed—not for them.

Bob became the focal point for the depression that both he and Dave suffered. On the surface at least, Dave never appeared to suffer from the affliction that overwhelmed Bob. In effect, Bob was used as a convenient receptacle for Dave's depression. Dave dumped his depression onto Bob instead of handling it himself.

In many ways, this was due to a more general aspect of their relationship. Dave and Bob were bound together emotionally. Neither was an independently functioning unit. As we shall see shortly, this is one of the main characteristics of dysfunctional systems: their members are so strongly bound together that it is often impossible to say where one leaves off and the other begins. Dysfunctional systems are also characterized by denial; their members vigorously deny that they are in need of help.

In PubCore's hour of need, its employees looked to Dave and Bob to provide clear leadership and support. PubCore's employees were hit just as hard by the loss of WorldVu. They, too, wondered how PubCore would survive. Above all, they wanted reassurance from their leaders.

As the days, weeks, months, and even years went by without clear action on the part of Dave and Bob, the fear and anxiety of PubCore's employees turned to anger and disgust. Their anger was a response to the feeling that they had been abandoned, and even betrayed, by those who should have taken better care of them, much as children need to be cared for and reassured by their parents in times of need. Dave and Bob couldn't attend to PubCore's crisis because they hadn't been trained, educated, or prepared to deal with the inevitable crises that life throws at everyone.

It wasn't a matter of their being bad, unethical, or uneducated. On the contrary, both were highly intelligent, well educated, and principled.

If anything, Dave and Bob were the victims of their own success. They had learned how to operate mainly in periods of growth. As a consequence, they had never really learned the benefits of strategic thinking and of questioning their fundamental business assumptions, which, it turned out, were only appropriate for good times. Furthermore, they had never understood that addressing mental health concerns may be appropriate not just for the seriously dysfunctional but for others as well. Thus, they had never laid the proper foundations for managing in difficult times.

Unfortunately, things only got worse. As the economy worsened in the late eighties and early nineties, PubCore failed to attract new business accounts. It ran up record operating deficits, with the inevitable consequence that PubCore's board of directors finally took over its day-to-day management. Dave was allowed to "retire gracefully." When it became apparent that Bob was no longer in the decision-making loop, he submitted his letter of resignation.

Would PubCore's demise have been avoided if both Bob and Dave had sought counseling? Can organizations in general avoid failure by paying more attention to the development and mental well-being of their employees? No one can say for sure because, unfortunately, there is still much that we don't know about the complexities of individuals and organizations, and few managers and executives understand how their own mental states affect and are affected by their work environments. But one thing is clear: we can no longer ignore the fact that there is a complex functional relationship between the mental health of individuals and that of organizations themselves.

The Emotions of Individuals

"In 1989, clinical depression cost U.S. employers $17 billion in time lost from work," reports an article in *American Demographics*, which goes on to say that according to the National Institute of Mental Health, one out of twenty American adults may be clinically depressed. The article continues:

> In 1988, 26 experienced interviewers met with 1,870 Westinghouse managers and professionals aged 25 to 55.
>
> They asked the 1,556 men and 314 women who volunteered for the study about depression, alcohol abuse and dependency, and family members who had mental illness.
>
> The study showed that few people recognized their own mental-health problems and that even fewer will seek help. . . . According to the study, 50% of those interviewed acknowledged having symptoms of depression. But few professionals or

managers would admit that they missed deadlines (14% did), that their work performance was affected by mental-health problems (6%), or that a manager (8%) or colleague (6%) had suggested counselling. Of the 24% of employees who had problems with alcohol sometime during their lives, only 5% of men and 19% of women ever sought help, according to the study.[1]

The article notes "a strong link between job conditions and mental health." For example, "the onset of employee depression is often associated with conflict with the supervisor."

In *Quiet Desperation: The Truth About Successful Men*, management consultant Jan Halper describes what she found after interviewing more than four thousand executives, managers, and professionals in Fortune 500 companies. More than 70 percent of her respondents lied to their subordinates about their poor performance instead of giving them honest and constructive criticism. In addition, 58 percent of middle managers and professionals whom she interviewed felt that they had wasted their lives in striving for, and even in achieving, goals that were basically "empty and meaningless."[2]

An articled called "Overstressed by Success" that appeared in *Newsweek* reported that a handful of experts are beginning to specialize in treating executives in distress. Among the reasons cited for executive stress was *encore anxiety*, or the fear of not being able to repeat or sustain earlier achievements. Some executives live in dread that the inadequacy they feel will be found out, and they compensate by driving themselves harder. The article also reports that "many troubled execs have molded their lives according to a distorted sense of what their parents or others expect from them."[3]

As these examples indicate, people are complex emotional beings. And without a doubt, the emotions of individuals have a strong impact on an organization's productivity. Indeed, many studies have shown a relationship between emotions, morale, and job performance. Further, none of the key programs of an organization, such as total quality management, can be accomplished without the emotional investment of virtually all the members of an organization. The best thinking and logic in the world will not improve organizations and individuals one iota, or induce them to get behind important programs, if participants are not committed on a deep emotional level. In sum, we need to more fully recognize the importance of emotional factors in the functioning of organizations.

We cannot expect to have healthy organizations without healthy employees. The opposite is also true. Individual health can only flourish within organizations and societies that are themselves healthy. Unfortunately, many organizations have deeply institutionalized sicknesses. In some cases sickness is not only a fundamental part of the culture but even a prerequisite for fitting in. For instance, psychotherapist Douglas LaBier, whose practice is devoted almost exclusively to the treatment of individuals who work in large organizations, found that many employees who were considered sick by their institutions were normal from a psychotherapeutic standpoint, while those who were considered normal, and hence were pointed to as role models by their organizations, in fact exhibited such serious psychological symptoms as lust for power, need to conquer others, feelings of grandiosity, destructiveness, and intense cravings for self-humiliation.[4]

What happens is that individuals and organizations become intertwined and enmeshed. The feelings, thoughts, and behaviors developed by individuals are reinforced by an organization's culture. If the culture is unhealthy or dysfunctional, it reinforces dysfunctional behaviors and emotions in the individual. In this way, the individuals in dysfunctional organizations and the organizations themselves become symbiotic, codependent. Dysfunctional organizations perpetuate and maintain themselves by attracting those who need them; in turn, the organization is perpetuated by the kinds of individuals it attracts and molds. The attractor mechanisms at work are both subtle and powerful.

Thus, although individual therapy may be helpful to employees in distress, it is not enough. Treatment must acknowledge and address the complex organizational system of which employees are a part. Organizations must also be "put on the couch."[5]

The Dysfunctions of Organizations

If modern organizations find it difficult to restructure themselves to make sense of the complex information they must handle, then they find it even more difficult to acknowledge that they are cauldrons and incubators for some of the most powerful and destructive human impulses. If it is difficult for families to admit that they are dysfunctional—whether they perpetrate physical, sexual, or emotional abuse—then it is even more difficult for organizations to acknowledge that they, too, are often dysfunctional systems. Yet, in the ways they treat employees, many organizations are similar to and sometimes worse than dysfunctional families. Examples that come immediately to mind are the incidents of sexual abuse and harassment that have engulfed many organizations such as the U.S. Congress and Navy in recent years.

While not all families and organizations are as dysfunctional as those of serious alcoholics, all possess some of the characteristics of such families. As identified by Anne Wilson Schaef and Diane Fassel, these include the following:

- *Denial.* The dysfunctional system denies it has a problem when others believe or can see clearly that it does. This is a major defense mechanism, maintaining the dysfunctional system as a closed system.

- *Confusion.* Dysfunctional systems are filled with inordinate amounts of confusion. This prevents everyone from taking responsibility not only for their actions but also for their maintenance of the system itself.

- *Self-centeredness.* Both the addict and the system are completely absorbed in themselves, thus denying the needs and feelings of others.

- *Perfectionism.* Individuals in dysfunctional systems desire to be perfect and, hence, are obsessed with not being "good enough."

- *Dishonesty.* The use of pathological lies is a characteristic of dysfunctional systems.

- *Scarcity model.* Dysfunctional members tend to compete with each other in the pursuit of money, time, and love.

- *Illusion of control.* Members of dysfunctional systems search for omnipotence.

- *Frozen feelings.* Members of dysfunctional systems are unable to be in touch with their basic feelings, intuition, and other vital sources of information that would allow them to see themselves and the system for what it is.

- *Ethical deterioration.* A result of being constantly immersed in a dysfunctional system is ethical deterioration.[6]

Other characteristics include depression, abnormal thinking processes, extreme dependency, extreme defensiveness, and a continuing crisis orientation toward every aspect of life.

We are not saying that there are no families or companies that are healthy.[7] We are merely saying that there are degrees and shades of health. Health, like disease, is complex. The fact is that much of what we know about seriously dysfunctional systems is applicable to somewhat healthy systems. Indeed, because dysfunctional systems are so extreme, studying them may actually help us identify the mechanisms necessary for health.

Through our work in crisis management, we have first-hand knowledge of and experience with serious organizational dysfunctions. The rationalizations that organizations use to deny their vulnerabilities to major crises provide strong and clear evidence of dysfunction and of the working of major defense and denial mechanisms. Mitroff, Pearson, and their colleagues conducted interviews with more than five hundred senior executives in more than two hundred organizations.[8] The respondents were generally the top individuals overseeing crisis management for their organizations. They were asked: Is crisis management taken seriously in your organization? What are the general beliefs in your organization that either support or inhibit effective crisis management? How would you describe the general culture of your organization? How does it either support or inhibit effective crisis management?

The responses to the questions clearly revealed that many organizations have adopted an exceedingly clever series of rationalizations to deny their need for crisis management (Table 4.1). Further, the responses also revealed that, in the vast majority of cases, we were not just dealing with individual beliefs but rather with the general mind set or culture of the entire organization. In nearly all cases, the interviewees responded as follows: Please understand me; what I'm going to say is *not* what I believe personally; rather, it is the general mind set of top management or what prevails around here.

No organization we observed subscribed to all of the rationalizations. However, the greater the number of rationalizations that were endorsed, the more vulnerable to crises, or crisis-prone, an organization was. Since the rationalizations are discussed more fully elsewhere, we shall not comment further on them here.[9] What is important to note is the fact that our study reveals that the characteristics of crisis-prone organizations are uncannily similar to those described by Shaef and Fassel.

The upshot is that organizational culture must, both in principle and in general, be considered a prime factor in the formation and maintenance of dysfunctional behaviors. The culture of an organization is the set of rarely articulated, largely unconscious, taken-for-granted beliefs, values, norms, and fundamental assumptions the organization makes about itself, the nature of people in general, and its environment.[10] In effect, organizational culture consists of the set of unwritten rules that govern acceptable behavior within and even outside of the organization. For instance, an organization's culture may prescribe such unwritten rules as: If you want to succeed around here, don't disagree with the boss; Don't be the bearer of bad news; or Don't share information with rival groups within the organization; your first loyalty is to your own immediate work group, not to others. On the other hand, innovative organizations have a positive culture that is revealed in norms such as: The best ideas are those that "rock the boat," or You won't be fired for making "creative" mistakes as long as you keep open lines of communication with superiors. Corporate culture affects what is considered ac-

TABLE 4.1. Faulty Rationalizations That Can Seriously Harm an Organization and Its Environment.

Group 1: Properties of the Organization That Will Protect It from Crises	Group 2: Properties of the Environment That Will Protect the Organization	Group 3: Properties of the Crises Themselves	Group 4: Policy-supporting Beliefs That Will Protect Us from Future Crises
1. Our size will protect us.	1. If a major crisis happens, someone else will rescue us.	1. Most crises turn out not to be very important.	1. Crisis management is like an insurance policy; you only need to buy so much.
2. Excellent, well-managed companies do not have crises.	2. Crisis management is someone else's responsibility.	2. Each crisis is so unique that it is not possible to prepare for them.	2. In a crisis situation, we just need to refer to the emergency procedures we've laid out in our crisis manuals.
3. Our special location will protect us.	3. The environment is benign, or we can effectively buffer ourselves from the environment.	3. Crises are solely negative in their impact.	3. We are a team that will function well during a crisis.
4. Certain crises only happen to others.	4. Nothing new has really occurred that warrants change.	4. Crises are isolated.	4. Only executives need to be aware of our crisis plans; why scare our employees or members of the community?
5. Crises do not require special procedures.	5. It's not a crisis if it doesn't happen to or hurt us.	5. Most if not all crises have a technical solution.	
6. It is enough to react to a crisis once it has happened.		6. It's enough to throw technical and financial quick fixes at a problem.	

7. Crisis management or crisis prevention is a luxury.

8. Employees who bring bad news deserve to be punished.

9. Desirable business ends justify high-risk means.

10. Our employees are so dedicated that we can trust them without question.

7. Most crises resolve themselves; therefore time is our best ally.

8. Crime/murder is just a cost of doing business.

5. The only important thing in crisis management is to make sure that our internal operations stay intact.

6. We are tough enough to react to a crisis in an objective and rational manner.

7. We know how to manipulate the media.

8. The most important thing in crisis management is to protect the good image of the organization through public relations and advertising campaigns.

Source: Christine M. Pearson and Ian I. Mitroff, "From Crisis Prone to Crisis Prepared: A Framework for Crisis Management," *The Executive*, 1993, 7(1), 48–59.

ceptable: styles of dress; proper models of talk and body language; how one socializes and with whom; who's considered a hero, villain, or victim; who's in and who's out; where to live; whom to marry; where to go to school; and with whom to eat lunch.

Since organizational culture is a major factor in the formation and maintenance of dysfunctional behaviors, then no wonder it is often so difficult to get those who are the prime bearers and representatives of an organization's culture to change significantly. Dysfunctional behaviors are not only reinforced daily but also rewarded overtly. Dysfunctional behavior is thus a prerequisite for initial membership, and it is also a major factor in promotion to high office. To change the individuals who work for such organizations therefore means changing the dysfunctional system of which they are a part, and vice versa.

Treating the System

While not perfect by any stretch of the imagination, individual and family therapies have learned how to treat individuals and whole families as collective systems. In the last ten years in particular, a great deal has been learned about treating individual and group dysfunctions ranging from incest and alcoholism to drug abuse and codependency. But as yet, very little of this knowledge has been extended to organizations.

One of the prominent discoveries about dysfunctional families—those, for instance, in which a member has a serious addictive disorder, such as alcoholism—is that the kinds of so-called solutions they adopt may actually reinforce the initial problem. In the case of alcoholism, it has been found that by constantly covering for the problem spouse, the husband or wife actually maintains the problem by keeping the system intact. In the literature of alcoholism, the spouse is called a *co-conspirator*. To really solve the problem, the whole system would have to change drastically.

By the same token, the vast majority of techniques that have been developed to change organizations—team building, empowerment, motivational uplifting—not only fail to solve the problem but may actually help maintain the dysfunctionality of the system. These techniques often merely touch the surface of emotional complexity and can only work in those organizations that are already somewhat healthy. In some cases, the adoption of these devices is more a symptom of the continuing commitment to disease than a step to organizational health. Such programs are often exceedingly effective in convincing organizations that they are attempting fundamental change when in fact they are not.

It is no longer sufficient for organizations to hire specialists in motivation, drug abuse, training, empowerment, and organizational change and development. In addition, techniques must be devised to get beneath the surface to the real source of the issues that prevent individuals and organizations from changing. Organizations must acknowledge that the process of change will be long, difficult, and extremely precarious. Dysfunctions reinforce one another as part of a total system. Until this is acknowledged and until treatment programs are formed that are based on the principles of treating dysfunctional systems *as systems*, there will be little success in helping individuals and organizations change.

We believe that there is a desperate need for serious programs set up to address the emotional issues of organizations. We believe that the problems from which they suffer and the forces that keep them locked into place are too serious to be treated with quick fixes. Because of the extreme emotional complexity of human beings and their associated institutions, mental health may require permanent, ongoing participation in specialized programs. Health is far too precious and precarious a matter to be left to chance.

In recent years, programs have been developed especially for the treatment of dysfunctional families—the Centers for Recovering Families, for example. We are convinced that equivalent kinds of major centers are needed for the treatment not only of recovering managers in organizations but also of the organizations themselves. In saying this, we are under no illusions that getting top managers and executives to admit openly that they are dysfunctional, or that they are seeking treatment and are willing to go through long processes of recovery, will be easy. Be this as it may, the situation is not impossible. In recent years, CEOs of major organizations have admitted that they and their top executives suffer from alcoholism. Thus, alcoholism—to cite one example—no longer carries the stigma it once did and is no longer a ground for dismissal, *if* an alcoholic admits the problem and is willing to undergo serious treatment. The same attitude is beginning to emerge with regard to more serious addictions, such as to hard drugs. Thus, it should be possible to adopt similar attitudes toward other addictions and dysfunctions from which managers and organizations suffer.

Envisioning the Recovery and Development Center

We believe that, in time, executives will see participation in programs of recovery and development as just as critical and just as important as learning the new knowledge skills that are necessary for managing organizations in a complex age. Recovery and development will be institutionalized and seen as one of the necessary aspects of organizational design.

The recovery and development center as we envision it has these major purposes:

- To help employees recover from whatever emotional dysfunctions or problems they bring with them to the organization, as well as those that invariably arise from being part of a complex organization, and to develop positive new ways of existing

- To help the organization as a whole recover from its systemic dysfunctions and develop into a healthy system

71

- To assess the top executives of the organization through personal interviews and with psychological instruments to determine the attractor mechanisms at work in recruiting and promoting them and to evaluate the impact of those mechanisms on their business decisions and on the key functions and programs of the organization

- To study and track over time the strength and persistence of the organization's rationalizations and general denial mechanisms to determine how they affect and interfere with key functions and programs

- To formulate and implement interventions and programs that are uniquely suited to the specific circumstances of the organization and that are truly effective in breaking the dysfunctions of the organization

- To supplement deep intervention and specialized programs with such traditional, surface-level techniques as team building, organizational development, and empowerment

When we refer to deep intervention and programs that are truly effective in breaking the dysfunctions of the organization, we have in mind something comparable in comprehensiveness and intensity to the twelve-step program of Alcoholics Anonymous. The twelve steps describe, in an archetypal way, a deep and long-lasting process of transformation. They can be applied effectively by individuals recovering from serious addictive disorders and can also be fruitfully extended to organizations themselves, as recent work has demonstrated and as we suggest in Chapter Seven.[11]

We know of an organization that cares for the homeless that has incorporated twelve-step principles into its day-to-day operations. The decision to have a permanent, ongoing twelve-step program was made in order to break down the distance and barriers between the executive staff of the organization and its clients. In the words of its president, "How dare we think we are 'better' than those we serve, that they are 'sick,' which they are in many cases, but that we are not!"[12]

We envision that the recovery and development dimension, like the knowledge and learning dimension, will have a permanent home and be headed by an officer who reports to the CEO. This officer will review daily the status of the organization's general health, interpreted and measured broadly. In particular, she or he will review the psychological strengths and weaknesses of the company's top management as revealed by tests, questionnaires, and key meetings that she or he has attended as an observer. This officer will assess how the internal conflicts of top management are getting in the way of the critical business decisions they must make as a group. The officer will also assess the strengths and weaknesses of the company's general culture, in particular by keeping a close watch on denial mechanisms and how they prevent the company from attending to the early warning signs of serious problems. She or he will also review the status and the nature of various treatment programs to help the company's top executives cope more effectively with their individual and group problems.

The paradox of the recovery and development dimension is that to deeply understand the dysfunctional aspects of the organization one must be both a member of the organization and outside of it at the very same time. The head and the members of the recovery program must be both (1) integral to and involved in the organization so that they can feel the full force of the dysfunction and (2) removed or distant enough from the organization so that they can see it for what it is. As a result, the members of the recovery program will have to constantly rotate in and out of it. They will have to have enough contact with the organization to know and to understand deeply its business, culture, mind set, dysfunctions, strengths, and language. At the same time, they must remove themselves from the organization to reflect on their own contamination by it. For this reason, the members will have to include external consultants and specialists in mental health who can help the employees of the recovery program as well as the organization itself.

Clearly, one of the most critical and important issues of all has to do with the ethics of requiring, if not forcing, the top executives of an organization to participate in a recovery program. No program in an organization can succeed without the blessing and deep commitment of the CEO and his or her top support staff. The CEO and that staff must not only support the recovery program but also participate in it. This requirement is justified, given the power of top management to affect the lives of employees, employee families, and the environment. Thus, part of the critical personal decision to become a member of top management will involve the decision to partake in an ongoing, permanent process of recovery and development.

The recovery dimension cannot work if it is completely subservient to a CEO and executive staff who ignore its diagnoses and block its effectiveness. For this reason, the recovery program will have to have direct access to the board of directors.

There is always the danger that the recovery program can become the "thought police" of an organization. For this reason, we believe that the concept can only work if there is recourse to an appeal mechanism to ensure that its judgments can be reversed if necessary.

In spite of its importance, we must acknowledge that the recovery dimension is still mainly at the recognition stage, if that. Organizations are only slowly beginning to realize that deeper actions on their part are called for if they are to become truly effective and continually adaptive. The organization that cares for the homeless that we mentioned earlier in this chapter is still the rare exception. Nonetheless, we believe that organizations will eventually come to institutionalize the concepts developed in this chapter.

In short, the attitude of Westinghouse must become common fare: "We want to be a leader," explained E. Carrol Curtis, corporate medical director for Westinghouse and the driving force behind the study mentioned earlier in this chapter. "We want total quality in our products and services and also in our people."[13]

FIVE

WORLD SERVICE
AND
SPIRITUALITY

The elements of the organizational design we have proposed so far acknowledge and meet the cognitive and emotional needs of those who live and work in organizations. As important as these are, they do not, however, meet all of the needs of human beings. Some of the deepest impulses of humankind are religious and spiritual. And people do not leave them at the door when they arrive at work. Such impulses seek expression and satisfaction in a variety of ways. They challenge an organization to tap into and promote the spiritual lives of employees by providing activities and programs that serve the world and thereby give broader meaning and purpose to life.

Spiritual Vision, Spiritual Blindness:
Two Stories

Mickey Weiss is a retired food executive. He worked some thirty-five years in the major food distribution strip of Los Angeles.[1] For the most part, his work life was uneventful. He did his job and that was that.

There were, however, signs along the way that Mickey was different. For instance, there was the time he commissioned an artist to paint a mural along one of the huge, blank, unattractive walls that faced the food strip. Because his fellow executives did not see the point of such a mural, they were unwilling to contribute monies to the project. So Mickey hired an artist on his own and paid for it himself.

The mural is a beautiful depiction of the entire food chain, from crops growing in the fertile valleys of central California through the arrival of food at the large urban centers. The mural is obviously about more than food and its transportation. It is about the fundamental miracle of food—of life itself—and the human situation that makes its growing and distribution possible.

The mural project was remarkable, but it was only a prelude to something even more so.

Not long after his retirement, Mickey went back to the food docks to clear up some business. While he was there, he happened to look at some crates of berries at the far end of the dock. Although still edible, the berries had ripened beyond the point where they could be sold to the major food chains. They no longer had the luster and appearance of first-class produce. Thus, they were destined to be trashed. For some reason, Mickey's gaze continued in a straight line across the street to a group of homeless people. Instantly, he made the connection. Instead of throwing out tons of perfectly good food every day, a way had to be found to get that food to those who were in desperate need of it. Mickey had found not only a new career but, more importantly, a new purpose— perhaps even a higher purpose.

Mickey's problem was only beginning. He was able to get the wholesalers to donate the food to him. It was destined to be trashed, after all. (The waste disposal companies were not exactly pleased with this, since their profits stood to suffer.) How to distribute all the food became the next challenge Mickey faced.

An angel in the form of the president of one of the major car rental companies came to the rescue. He agreed to rent to Mickey a fleet of small vans for the price of one dollar per vehicle per week.

It then occurred to Mickey that there was nothing unique or special about Los Angeles. The same situation must exist throughout the entire country. How, then, could one form a network of programs across the United States?

With this realization, Mickey sensed he needed help. He contacted the Annenberg School of Communication at the University of Southern California. Mickey didn't know it at the time, but the Annenberg School has some of the world's leading scholars concerned with the spread of social innovations across and throughout societies. Subsequently, the dean of the school and several scholars decided to adopt Mickey's project.

Mickey and his new colleagues at USC are currently exploring ways to get other cities to adopt the same kind of program. He is running into all kinds of problems that typically plague good social innovations. In some locales, for example, public officials do not want to come to a national conference because they do not like having representatives of the homeless in their and other cities. In addition, there is resistance to ideas that are invented elsewhere.

By way of contrast, consider another example. On the local TV news one night, sandwiched between the earth-shaking and the banal, were shots of a huge trash bin located behind a Footlocker store in Los Angeles. In the bin were scores of new-looking running shoes that had been severely slashed so that they could no longer be worn. The reporter asked the obvious question: With the plight of the homeless so evident in our society, why hadn't the store or the company donated the shoes to charities to aid the unclothed? What, if anything, would the store have lost by doing this?

At first, the only feeble excuse, which itself had to be dragged from the company, was that the shoes were old, abandoned models and might not be safe for use. Thus, to lessen the possibility of legal liability, the company not only disposed of the shoes but had them deliberately slashed so that they could not be worn. Later, however, the company seemed to realize its error and said that in the future it would donate shoes to an appropriate charity.

The incident was not a major news story or event. No

one was killed, maimed, raped, or shot, as happens daily in Los Angeles. And yet the incident raised significant questions. Would a truly caring, compassionate, and moral society, let alone a single company, have allowed such a thing to occur? If a company can be said to think, then what was it thinking—or better yet, not thinking—in order for something like this to occur? Who gave the order, issued the policy directive, wrote the memo, made the telephone call, or undertook the action—perhaps on their own—to destroy shoes that could have given warmth, comfort, and even a small piece of dignity to another fellow human being? Was the incident just another symptom of the bureaucratic numbness and dumbness of present-day corporate America?

The stories of Mickey Weiss and the Footlocker store illustrate the fundamental importance of connections. When connections are made—connections between the small self and the larger world, between human needs and potential solutions—spiritual vision is at work. When such connections are not made, it is due to spiritual blindness.

Spiritual Connections

What is the essence of spirituality in organizations? It is this: to encourage and allow everyone involved with an organization to draw his or her own unique spiritual connections between the resources of that organization and an important social or environmental problem that those resources could help to alleviate. Sadly, it is often easier to demonstrate cases where this does not happen than where it does. Thus, for instance, C. West Churchman recounts his experience with the CEO of a major soft drink company. Since the company was a leader in marketing soft drinks around the world, Churchman asked the CEO whether this same marketing apparatus could be used to distribute food to the needy. The CEO barked back angrily, "That's not our business!"[2] This response is not only unwarranted but also illustrative of the moral and spiritual emptiness that exists in many organizations. It breaks the connection between an organization and the rest of humanity.

Fundamentally, spirituality is a special act of recognition, the recognition that there is a connection between one's everyday affairs or business and humanity's problems. This is exemplified in Mickey's story. Surely, countless other executives had looked at crates of food waiting to be discarded, and yet they never made the connection. Mickey himself didn't make it until for some reason he was ready for it. What Mickey did then can only be described as a profoundly moral and spiritual act. He made a *moral and spiritual connection* between crates of food that were destined to be trashed and those who could most use it. Further, he not only acted on his new moral and spiritual connection or principle, but he generalized it to all of humanity.

Spirituality in organizations is also concerned with the development and nourishment of the human energy that is necessary to accomplish all tasks great and small. Indeed, nothing great or small can be accomplished without inner spirit or inspiration, which the dictionary tells us is derived from two words: *ens*, or within, and *spiritus*, or God. Thus, to be inspired is literally to follow or to be in contact with one's "God within."

To propose a new product idea or service, champion it through an organization, overcome endless and needless delays and difficulties, persist in the face of a thousand hurdles and indignities, preserve one's sanity, keep one's mental well-being alive—all these and more require spirit. How, indeed, can world-class products be developed and services be performed without animation, courage, liveliness, mettle, and vigor? Whatever terms are used to describe what is needed, they are nothing but spirit in disguise.

In many organizations, unfortunately, the expression of spiritual impulses—or even the acknowledgment of them—is either strictly forbidden or trivialized. One is asked variously to

- Deny them altogether

- Suppress and repress them

- Put them aside

- Express them elsewhere on one's own time

- Put them down, devalue them, or ridicule them

- Judge them inappropriate

- Minimize them by interpreting spirituality to mean company spirit or enthusiasm

Through such means, we fragment our existence. We experience anomie. We accept an incredible number of disconnects and separations in our lives. And the more we accept, the easier it becomes to accept others until, finally, we are no longer full human beings. We have shrunk and bounded our very experience. We have become spiritually blind. But no organization can succeed today whose employees have such a narrow vision. We need to open up, to broaden the ways in which we perceive ourselves and the world.

We want to emphasize that the recognition of spirituality in organizations does not mean compelling workers to accept an official company religion or forcing them to participate in one of the world's major religions. It does mean encouraging each worker to give something back to the broader environment. This is the sense in which we speak of spirituality.

Some organizations are incorporating or working to incorporate spirituality, whether they know it or not, in the form of corporate giving and environmental programs. Corporate giving seeks to enhance the human community in which a company is located, while environmentalism aims to protect the natural environment. Both types of programs make connections. It may not be obvious that spiritual impulses are involved in environmentalism, but scholars are beginning to acknowledge that the contemporary environmental movement is essentially a modern religious or spiritual movement.[3] No organization can mount a serious program of environmentalism—or of corporate giving, for that matter—if it does not recognize that religious and spiritual impulses are present and must be dealt with at some point.

The Moral Imperative

As is probably evident from what we've said thus far in this chapter, we believe that organizations have a fundamental moral and ethical responsibility to continually develop new programs, and to allow their employees to work on programs, that serve such broader human needs as the care and feeding of the needy and the abatement of environmental pollution. Where does such an imperative come from? It begins in the sense of moral outrage that we feel when we hear about something like the Footlocker episode. It begins in the outrage expressed in questions like, How dare they [we] do such things [or not do them]? (For instance, how could Exxon have allowed a captain with a clear and repeated record of drinking to pilot a ship in so critical a region as Prince William Sound and by so doing pollute one of the most beautiful and fragile corners of the environment?)

The moral imperative grows when we realize that our actions in the world can and do make a difference. Here we move into the realm of theology and philosophy, and look anew at the debate between free will and determinism that raged in the nineteenth century. We find the concept of God developed by one of America's greatest philosophers, William James, particularly helpful in building a foundation for the moral imperative.

James's concept of God starts with wondering how, if God is perfect and all-knowing, we can account for the undeniable presence of evil in the world. After all, God could have chosen to make us all a little bit more complete, less blind, less one-sided in our development, more integrative, and so on.

Carl Jung once suggested—in the spirit of his chosen profession, psychoanalysis—that perhaps God, too, has an unconscious or blind side that precludes knowledge of all the consequences of God's plans or actions. James went even further. He suggested that God's powers are limited so that humankind is free to develop and exercise moral choice. In James's view, the world is not complete. Humankind's actions therefore make a *real difference* in the outcome of the world. In a passage that is especially revealing, James states his position quite clearly:

> Suppose the author of the world put this case to you at the very moment of creation: "I am going to make a world not certain to be saved, a world the perfection of which shall be conditioned merely, the condition that each . . . agent does its own level best. I offer you the chance of taking part in such a world. Its safety, you see, is [not certain]. It is a real adventure, with real danger, yet it may win through. It is a social scheme of cooperative work genuinely to be done. Will you join the procession? Will you trust yourself and trust the other agents enough to face the risk?[4]

From this perspective, humankind has a fundamental moral imperative to work on behalf of bettering the world and thereby itself. Once one admits that human beings have no choice but to play a fundamental role in shaping themselves and the world, a secondary issue of design then becomes paramount. That is, how do we want to design our work lives, our organizations, our world?

This question takes on a special urgency in our era. For the first time in history, human-induced crises such as Bhopal, Chernobyl, and Exxon Valdez have the potential to rival natural disasters and forces in their scope and magnitude.[5] If this capability were ever wedded to the evil side of the human psyche, humankind could produce changes larger and more destructive than anything brought on by the earth itself. The recent war in the Persian Gulf is a vivid testament to the capability of humans to alter the environment of the planet.

If our capacity to bring about large-scale destructive change is great, so also is our responsibility not to. Humankind has been thrust into the role of the major designer and shaper of the earth's fate. There is no way to escape this responsibility and, along with it, our moral and ethical obligation to build a healthier society and world.

In Search of Meaning

The spiritual side of organizations can no longer be denied or neglected. And yet, among those who study and describe organizations, their spiritual aspect is almost never acknowledged or treated seriously. This is due to the nature of conventional theories that underlie thinking about organizations—theories that fail to take into account the human hunger for meaning and thus miss something crucial, vital, and fundamental about organizational life.

To an overwhelming extent, most explanations and theories of organizations are *structural*. That is, the emphasis is on finding the right forms, the right boxes, or the right structures for organizations. Thus, a major assumption is that the behavior of organizations can be explained in terms of their structure, or that organizational behavior follows from structure. No consideration is given to purpose or meaning.

Even when purpose is acknowledged, it is most often expressed in terms of serving narrow goals, such as increasing stockholder equity or wealth. When the notion of purpose has been expanded to include broader goals, such as preserving and enhancing the environment, it is viewed as being on shaky ground; supposedly, while there can be a science of structure, there cannot be a science of purpose.

Earlier in this century, the philosopher E. A. Singer, one of William James's best students and a founder of pragmatism, showed that structure and purpose are not necessarily in conflict. They are merely ways of describing different aspects of the same thing. Thus, structural and purposeful descriptions of nature, or of organizations, are not necessarily in conflict.

In a brilliant paper, Singer showed that mechanical explanations of the world, which see behavior as a purely physical process and which imply that all our actions are determined, are *not* inherently incompatible with teleological or purpose-based explanations, which posit that behavior is directed toward an end or shaped by a purpose and which imply that our actions and our wills are free.[6] For example, a person skydiving is subject to both mechanical and teleological explanations. Insofar as one is falling, the movement of one's body and where one lands are determined by the laws of physics of mechanics. In this respect, one has no choice, and, hence, one's behavior is determined. However, the decision to jump out of an airplane is presumably purposeful and subject to the individual's own choice.

Singer left the impression that a combination of mechanics and teleology is sufficient to explain the world. And, to an overwhelming extent, these are the explanations that are accepted by the scientific community and, especially, by those who study and describe organizations. But we question whether what we call spirituality can be reduced to one of Singer's types of scientific explanation. We ask, with William James, "Why, after all, may not the world be so complex as to consist of many interpenetrating spheres of reality, which we can thus approach in alternation by using different conceptions and assuming different attitudes? . . . In this view religion and science, each verified in its own way from hour to hour and from life to life, would be co-eternal."[7]

Spiritual experiences are a state of mind, a quality of being, a way of infusing one's life, one's work, with ultimate purpose and meaning. The sad fact is that for many in organizations, work does not contribute meaning to their lives. This situation must change.

Envisioning the World Service and Spirituality Center

The world service and spirituality center exists to encourage members of an organization to spend a portion of their work time on programs that are of service to humanity's greater needs: ending world hunger, preventing child abuse, addressing the problems of homelessness and poverty, encouraging community health, developing the arts, preventing war, and restoring the environment.

The world service and spirituality center as we envision it has these major purposes:

- To broaden the vision of the organization and its members

- To draw connections between (1) the critical skills and knowledge that every organization possesses and uses to conduct its "normal" operations and businesses and (2) world problems to which the organization's special skills and knowledge can be applied

- To infuse the organization and its members with the aliveness, enthusiasm, and spirit that are needed to reach true excellence

- To give the organization and its members a true sense of meaning and purpose

- To allow all members to work, on company time, on a world problem of importance to them

- To keep a company-wide record of the individual projects that its members are working on so that synergy can be achieved wherever possible

- To monitor and acknowledge the wrongdoings that one's organization has committed in the past, is committing in the present, or is about to commit, and to make it a central focus of one's mission to eliminate them

In conjunction with the last of these purposes, we should note that it is not enough to do good in the world; the organization must also refrain from doing evil. Thus, if its corporate mission (or the means of attaining it) is corrupt, no amount of money given to charity will make employees feel that their work is meaningful or spiritually satisfying. Ideally, the corporate mission of an organization, and not just one or two of its programs, should be in service to humanity's greater needs.

We have met more than one engineer who made the conscious decision to leave the aerospace defense industry to go to work for the Disney corporation because they could not justify to themselves or their families what they did for a living. More than one engineer with whom we have talked said, and almost in these exact words: I can bring my family to Disneyland and say with pride, "I designed that ride."

We should also note that when an organization turns its attention to world problems, it soon becomes evident that not only is each problem related to virtually all other problems in ways we do not understand completely, but each also seems to be contained in and a fundamental part of all other problems in ways that we do not fully comprehend. For example, Mickey Weiss's problem was intertwined not only with the problems of transportation and distribution but also with the business and economics of waste disposal, the general problem of homelessness, the problems of home ownership and rental, social services for the downtrodden, the growing inequity between the haves and the have-nots, and on and on. This is why it is so important to look for synergy between programs.

The world service and spirituality center, like the other centers we have discussed, will have a home and a chief officer. The officer will review the status of the various individual and social programs that the company's employees have chosen to adopt and use in order to improve the world. Some may be volunteers at centers for abused children; some may prepare meals for the homeless; the possibilities are endless. The officer will help employees determine where their energies and corporate donations should be dedicated and will also coordinate the natural synergy that may exist between programs. The officer will be responsible for eliminating potential conflicts and unethical programs altogether.

Every organization, no matter what its business, is in the position to make a contribution of some kind to help alleviate the world's problems or increase the world's awareness. There are as many ways to give as there are organizations. By way of illustration, we'll end this chapter by describing how two different companies are making a contribution.

Three Companies Give Back

The Body Shop sells cosmetics, but it does so with a conscience. It obtains many of its ingredients in a nonexploitative way from developing countries around the world. It does not test on animals. And it requires its employees to give time every week to social or environmental causes of their choice.

A newspaper article recently described the very different way another business has chosen to make connections:

> Newly situated above one of Los Angeles' busiest street corners, [a] $75,000 computerized sign burned with two graphic reminders of a troubled world: "ACRES OF RAIN FOREST NOW . . . 1,996,362,331. WORLD POPULATION NOW . . . 5,401,201,514."
>
> Each second, the rain forest total ticked downward by one—and the world population jumped by nearly three.
>
> The sign—on the facade of the Hard Rock Café at Beverly and La Cienega Boulevards—is the brainchild of café owner Peter Morton, 44, who has made environmentalism a part of his entrepreneurial wisdom. A board member of the Natural Resources Defense Council, Morton hit upon the idea of the sign last summer and spent six months having it constructed to fit the well-known eatery—heretofore most conspicuous for the tailfin, '59 Cadillac jutting from its roof. . . .

The telephonic response so far to the running tally has been extraordinary—thousands of telephone calls, according to Morton, who began using the phrase "Save the Planet" in the Hard Rock Café logo 15 years ago.

"A lot of people have already asked us, 'What can we do?'" Morton said. "We're saying, 'The best thing you can do is to donate money to organizations that are working directly to preserve the rain forests.'"[8]

The giant multinational firm CIBA-GEIBY found yet another way to give back. It asked of itself: How can we get our pharmaceutical drugs to those who are in desperate need of them and not merely to those who can afford to pay for them? Having asked itself this crucial question, it ultimately made the decision to sell its drugs in Africa even though it would only make a profit of 1 to 2 percent, an amount that was substantially below its usual rates of return. To justify this low rate of return, it reasoned as follows: If we sell our drugs in Africa, we will build our reputation in the eyes of the world as a company that really cares and wants to help. We can thus factor this in as a positive amount on our bottom line. If we do, and further, if we estimate what this amount would be, our operations in Africa will then be in line with our other business units and their rates of return. Therefore, we ought to do so!

Notice that in promoting a nontraditional business goal, CIBA-GEIGY was pioneering a new concept of accounting, which some have come to call *environmental account-*

ing. We would prefer, however, to call it *world service accounting*. World service accounting is concerned fundamentally with developing new measures of economic performance that will allow firms to engage in humanitarian acts that traditional accounting practices would discourage, if not forbid entirely. This practice reflects the spiritual dimension in the best sense of the term.

SIX

WORLD-CLASS
OPERATIONS

We have considered the importance of recognizing and meeting employees' cognitive, emotional, and spiritual needs. This is not only to support health as an end in itself but also to enable implementation of world-class manufacturing or service operations. As much as manufacturing a product or rendering a service, the world-class operations dimension is also concerned with continually reinventing the organization itself by incorporating the latest thinking about technology, service, and the nature and structure of organizations.

A Tale of Two Automobiles

It used to be that when an American bought a Ford, he or she could bet that every last nut and bolt head had been manufactured by Ford and assembled by Ford—indeed, that the metal for it had even been mined by Ford. Henry Ford believed that all of the major activities that went into manufacturing a Ford Motor Company product had to be controlled or owned by him, and, to the extent possible, products should be forged together at a single site. He wanted every critical resource that flowed into and out of his plants to be under his direct influence. The Ford plants at Highland Park (home of the Model T) and River Rouge ("the factory to end all factories") were emblematic of this model of manufacturing operations, which emphasized centralization and control.

Ford's biographers, Nevins and Hill, describe how the company had been developed by 1926:

> Raw materials were now flowing from the iron mines and lumber mills of the Upper Peninsula, from Ford coal mines in Kentucky and West Virginia, and from Ford glass plants in Pennsylvania and Minnesota, much of the product traveling on Ford ships or over Ford-owned rails. Ford's manufacture of parts had been expanded—starters and generators, batteries, tires, artificial leather, cloth, and wire had been manufactured by the company in increasing quantities. The Rouge was producing coke, iron, steel, bodies, castings, engines, and other elements for Highland Park and the assembly plants, and also manufacturing the full quota of [Ford tractors].[1]

Highland Park and River Rouge were tangible testaments to Ford's concept of organizational fusion. They became America's industrial cathedrals, enshrining the idea that the way to success was via a single, solid, mass production assembly line. Ford's competitor, Alfred P. Sloan, together with Pierre du Pont, Donaldson Brown, and others at General Motors, developed the multidivisional, multifunctional organizational form—the M-form we referred to in Chapter One—to manage the far-flung and monolithic activities characteristic of this way of doing business. Its combination of organizational principles and technology offered an enormous increase in the efficiency of large-scale operations and realized the exceptional returns that economists call "economies of scale," enabling the emergence of early twentieth-century industry.

Times have changed dramatically. Organizational fusion has given way to organizational fission as firms have sought ways to spin off business operations at which they do not excel. The auto industry that was once so tightly clustered has become broadly dispersed. Robert Reich, a political economist and secretary of labor in the Clinton administration, observes:

> When an American buys a Pontiac Le Mans from General Motors, for example, he or she engages unwittingly in an international transaction. Of the $20,000 paid to GM, about $6,000 goes to South Korea for routine labor and assembly operations, $3,500 to Japan for advanced components (en-

gines, transaxles, and electronics), $1,500 to West Germany for styling and design engineering, $800 to Taiwan, Singapore, and Japan for small components, $500 to Britain for advertising and marketing services, and about $100 to Ireland and Barbados for data processing. The rest—less than $8,000—goes to strategists in Detroit, lawyers and bankers in New York, lobbyists in Washington, insurance and health-care workers all over the country, and General Motors shareholders—most of whom live in the United States, but an increasing number of whom are foreign nationals.[2]

The fundamental assumption underlying the model of organizational success embraced by Henry Ford and Alfred Sloan was that the central activities of an organization should be concentrated tightly into a single, unified whole, and held under the ownership or direct control of the organization. Preferably all activities should be located at the same physical site. If the foregoing requirements were met, a firm would gain greater value from its activities. The firm would not only obtain maximum value from its markets but at the same time would keep its costs in line.

The end these pioneers had in mind—creating economic value by satisfying demand at minimal cost—is, of course, still valid today; but the means for achieving it are not. Massive changes in transportation and information technology and the emergence of the global economy make possible new options and demand new approaches. Organizations are beginning to think in terms of designing globally dispersed *systems* that create the maximum amount of net value. To understand this new thinking, let us start by examining at a fundamental level how the activities of an organization turn its vision into reality.

Turning Vision into Reality

The design of any organizational system starts with a clear vision of the products and services the organization will deliver to its customers. This vision must be, in the words of Burt Nanus, "a realistic, credible, attractive future for your organization." Henry Ford, for example, had a vision of a simple, functional automobile that was affordable for most Americans. David Sarnoff envisioned a "radio music box." "I have in mind," he wrote in a memorandum dated September 30, 1915, to the general manager of the Marconi Wireless Telegraph Company of America (a predecessor of RCA), "a plan of development which would make radio a 'household utility' in the same sense as the piano or phonograph. The idea is to bring music into the house by wireless."[3]

George David, the CEO of Otis Elevator, sums up his vision for his company as follows: "The only good elevator is an unnoticed one. Our objective is to go unnoticed." Ralph Lettieri, executive vice president of Benjamin Moore Paints, casts his vision like this: "I wanted the customer to be able to walk into a home decoration center with a sample of color and walk out again with paint that exactly matched the sample."

Ray Kroc believed that the concepts and assembly-line efficiencies pioneered by Henry Ford could be applied to popular foods such as hamburgers, french fries, and milk shakes. His vision became McDonald's. Walt Disney dreamed that people would enjoy attending an amusement park that was dressed up as a fantasy world. Thus Disneyland was born. Steve Jobs envisioned a small desktop computer for personal use. Apple Computer was the result. Anita Roddick wanted products that were good not only for women's bodies but for the environment as well. That vision yielded the Body Shop.

Organizations exist so that visions can be realized. An organization can be viewed as a complex sequence of value-adding activities that work together to achieve a vision. Each activity receives inputs, performs transforming processes on them, and produces outputs that can be sent to other activities for further processing. Each activity also involves the acquisition and consumption of resources—raw materials, labor, money, equipment, buildings, land, administration, supervision—and thereby creates costs. The ultimate value and cost of the final output delivered to the customer is the collective result of all of these activities. For this reason, the sequence of activities required to produce a business's products and services—those needed to pursue its vision—is called its *value chain*.

Most businesses have hundreds—even thousands—of activities in their value chains. These activities encompass obtaining raw materials, processing, distribution, marketing and sales, customer service, finance, human resources, research and development, planning, product design, advertising, administration, government relations, legal services, technology development, and gathering competitive intelligence. This list, of course, could be expanded, and each item could, in turn, be subdivided into smaller activities. The point is that each activity adds value to the organization's ultimate output and contributes to turning the organization's vision into reality.

Organizational Fission

Organizations that attempt to fuse the majority of activities in their value chains into a single, tightly concentrated line, as Ford did, are highly vulnerable in today's fast-paced, highly competitive global economy. As a result, the designers of modern organizations must challenge the assumption of centralization.

The designers of today's organizations must recognize that, in principle, any of a business's activities can be performed anywhere in the world by anyone who is best suited for the task, whether an employee of the organization or not. Indeed, if an organization is to achieve world-class performance, each of its activities should be performed in that part of the world that offers maximum value for it. This is not as outlandish a proposition as it might at first appear. Modern transportation and information systems provide a remarkable geographical range and scope within which any activity might productively be performed.

One key to designing a structure for world-class operations is to find the best place in the world in which to perform each of an organization's major activities. Generally speaking, any activity can be performed at any latitude and longitude on the globe. In practice, it will be performed in a country, city, or other geopolitical unit that has some kind of comparative advantage when it comes to adding value in a particular activity. A second key is to reduce the organization's ownership and control to just those activities that it performs best—its *core competencies*—and enter into agreements with others who can perform non-core activities better. These two efforts result in a *disaggregated* value chain.

A variety of arrangements have been used by firms to disaggregate their value chains. In these strategic alliances, as they can be called, one organization forms coalitions with other organizations so that it can realize its vision. Strategic alliances run the gamut from enforceable contracts to simple verbal agreements. The point is to secure world-class competency in an activity without having to own or construct it. As designers of organizations are starting to realize, an organization need not own every node (or even most of them) in its value-added network as long as each node delivers high-quality output on time and in keeping with cost objectives.

In fact, there are several reasons why, in the global environment, alliances are actually preferable to ownership. One is that alliances offer special capabilities that an organization might not otherwise acquire. Alliances can be formed or disbanded quickly, depending on changes in market conditions. They also offer advantages relating to control. Responsibilities can be pinpointed clearly. As economist Oliver Williamson suggests, by forming a few well-chosen alliances an organization can use competitive pressure among alternative external nodes in its network to hold down its costs and manage its risks.[4]

Two terms are commonly associated with the idea of strategic alliances. *Sourcing* refers to the process of securing a source of supply for some basic component or product in the organization's product line. Apple Computer, for example, buys its laser printer engines from Canon, a very successful Japan-based global company. Canon enjoys a fine reputation for world-class quality in printer engines and similar components. By using Canon's engine, Apple has managed some of its exposure to obsolescence risk in a field that changes rapidly. Meanwhile, Apple enjoys an assured, high-quality source of supply for an important complementary product without diluting its technical or financial resources on a technology it considers to be secondary to its core competency, which is controlling the "look and feel" of its Macintosh computers.

Outsourcing generally involves contracting with another organization to perform a value-adding activity. The activity is performed by the organization that bids to provide the most value for the cost. Economists have long argued that successive exchanges among activities in a firm's value chain should be mediated by market forces. Outsourcing, in effect, satisfies this requirement by allocating an activity to the organization that is best qualified to perform it. For example, data processing and information services are now frequently being outsourced to companies like Electronic Data Systems, Anderson Consulting, and IBM.

Increasingly, successful firms are disaggregating their value chains by sourcing and outsourcing and by distributing more of the activities over a broader geographical expanse. Robert Reich provides several key examples of what he calls the *global web*:

> Precision ice hockey equipment is designed in Sweden, financed in Canada, and assembled in Cleveland and Denmark for distribution in North America and Europe, respectively, out of alloys whose molecular structure was researched and patented in Delaware and fabricated in Japan. An advertising campaign is conceived in Britain and edited in New York. A sports car is financed in Japan, designed in Italy, and assembled in Indiana, Mexico, and France, using advanced electronic components invented in New Jersey and fabricated in Japan. A microprocessor is designed in California and financed in America and West Germany, containing dynamic random-access memories fabricated in South Korea. A jet airplane is designed in the state of Washington and in Japan, assembled in Seattle, with tail cones from Canada, special tail sections from China and Italy, and engines from Britain. A space satellite designed in California, manufactured in France, and financed by Australians is launched from a rocket made in the (former) Soviet Union.[5]

This new line of thinking has led to interesting and different corporate configurations. Take, for example, Sun

Microsystems. When Sun experienced almost insurmountable difficulties meeting its shipment deadlines for workstations, it finally took a drastic action. Sun jettisoned its eighteen distribution centers around the world and contracted with Federal Express and other carriers to take over its distribution function. The company is now setting shipment records. Even the value chain for one of Sun's lead products, the Sparc microprocessor, has been disaggregated. Fujitsu, Texas Instruments, and Cypress Semiconductors make specialized chips for the company under a licensing agreement. Solectron Corporation performs most of the manufacturing activities. And Bell Atlantic Business Systems Services, Eastman Kodak, and other companies with field engineering forces actually do the repairs on its machines in the field. The results are impressive. According to *Business Week*, "Sun's 12,800 employees generate $280,000 each in annual sales, topping all but Silicon Graphics Inc. in the workstation market and putting Sun in a different league from, say, IBM, which gets $188,000 per employee. A simple corporate commandment sums up Sun's philosophy: 'Thou shalt not do thyself what others can do better.' "[6]

A similar commandment has guided Lewis Galoob Toys. Headquartered in San Francisco, Galoob Toys recorded sales of about $127 million on assets of approximately $75 million in 1990. Micro Machines®, mini-vehicles, dolls, games, and Game Genie™ are among the products it sells worldwide, although the majority of its revenues come from North America and Europe. In addition to a very few of its own lead designers and engineers, the company engages independent designers and engineers all over the world, wherever anyone has the creative talent to design a new toy. Galoob produces virtually all of its products under proprietary and character licenses obtained from toy inventors and designers located around the globe. Some forty partner factories in Hong Kong, Thailand, and the People's Republic of China manufacture Galoob's products. To reduce the risk of losses due to political or economic disruptions in the countries where the manufacturing of Galoob's products occurs, Galoob purchased a forty-million-dollar insurance policy from Lloyd's of London. For all of this global capability, Galoob relies on just 100 employees of its own and about 199 more who operate its wholly owned Hong Kong subsidiary. This means that its sales per employee exceed $420,000. All other activities are performed by a widely dispersed network of small organizations and individuals with whom Galoob has negotiated contracts and license agreements.

Recently Galoob's stock has been depressed as the company sorts out patent infringement problems with several of its electronic games. There is an important management lesson in this. Although a company can realize substantial economic gains by disaggregating its value chain, it cannot totally absolve itself of all the liabilities associated with all the value-adding activities that become part of its broader network. Once again, an organization needs to be aware of and coordinate the innumerable assumptions that underlie its operations.

Perhaps the most fully disaggregated company today is the Rosenbluth International Alliance (RIA), a brainchild of travel agency executive Hal Rosenbluth. He calls RIA a *global virtual corporation*. The Rosenbluth business was founded in 1892 by Hal's great-grandfather, Marcus Rosenbluth, to provide transportation for immigrants from Europe to the United States via steamship. By 1974, Rosenbluth had become the largest and strongest travel agency in the Philadelphia area. When Hal joined the company, its sales were on the order of $20 million. Within a few years, Hal saw a new customer need and a great business opportunity. Rosenbluth Inc. was a regional travel agency, but many of its corporate customers were traveling all over the globe. The more he looked into it, the more Hal became convinced that global travel was increasing and that there was a need to manage it better. The people who managed travel for Rosenbluth's corporate clients were faced with the problems of consolidating worldwide travel, improving the management of travel information, reducing the costs of global travel, and improving services to business travelers worldwide. Rosenbluth's response was to form RIA, which is actually a partnership of travel management firms around the world that works to serve combined corporate accounts through information sharing, pooled negotiating clout, and cooperative customer service. The alliance only admits one travel management firm from each major world market, and every new member must satisfy such criteria as strong service orientation, a long history of financial health, a well-trained and respected leadership and staff, a commitment to information technology, and an elusive but crucial factor: cultural compatibility. That is, the candidate firm's philosophy, values, and dedication to client service must closely match Rosenbluth's.

RIA's central tenet is that travelers are provided the same services no matter where they are in the world. A customer who bought a ticket in London to travel to Tokyo can, upon arriving in Tokyo, call a number and get, for example, help in relocating to another hotel or in rebooking a flight to include a stopover in Hong Kong. Local assistance in English is available worldwide. The business traveler's employer also gets special savings and travel management reports. To the traveler and travel manager, everything is conducted as though all services were being delivered by one monolithic corporation. Behind the scenes, however, there is substantial disaggregation. About thirty-nine countries are served by thirty-four RIA partners with more than eleven hundred offices around the globe, united by a single information system.

The core competencies that Rosenbluth brings to the game are a global information system and the company's exceptional brokerage and coordination skills. Information technology provides global access to client itineraries and profiles by any member office, permits client participation in RIA's preferred-rate program, and supports the global consolidation of travel information. It is also used to monitor and control the performance of the alliance and its individual members on global accounts and special-rate programs.

RIA is managed by several standing committees, composed of members of the alliance, which focus on business areas such as industry relations, hotel accommodations, and a crucial trio called front office, middle room, and back office. RIA's strategy and plans are established by the entire membership. Decision making is by consensus whenever possible. Formal decisions are made on a one-member, one-vote basis regardless of the size of the participating member. RIA's budget, however, is funded by members based on the size of their revenues and assets. The committees are guided by several agreed-upon goals that are fundamental to RIA's vision as a global virtual corporation. Primary among these is that all members will agree to a single contract that permits them to define RIA's products and the common methods of receiving and disbursing money worldwide.

Rosenbluth's financial results are dazzling, due in large part to RIA's outstanding performance. Revenues grew from $20 million in 1976 to $1.5 *billion* in 1991—a growth rate of 7,500 percent. In 1992, the revenues generated by the company's 2,500 employees were about $600,000 per capita.[7]

Reinventing the Corporation

World-class operations require never-ending attention to knowledge acquisition, research, and innovation. "The most important invention that will come out of the corporate research lab in the future," observes Xerox's corporate vice president, John Seely Brown, "will be the corporation itself. As companies try to keep pace with rapid changes in technology and cope with increasingly unstable business environments, the research department has to do more than simply innovate new products. It must design the new technological and organizational 'architectures' that make possible a continuously innovating company. But another way, corporate research must reinvent innovation."[8]

Reinventing innovation, however, requires overcoming the formidable barriers that prevent organizations as a whole from learning. Primary among these are old habits of thought. It is a normal human instinct to protect one's way of life, and this is usually done by avoiding new thoughts, which almost by definition are dangerous. Thus, one begins the process of learning and knowledge acquisition "by challenging the implicit assumptions that have shaped the way people in an organization have historically looked at things."[9] The secret to this for Brown is to co-produce innovations by forming partnerships and "knowledge links" with people throughout an organization and with major external partners and stakeholders, especially customers. Not only must old assumptions be challenged but new methods are also required to communicate and exchange innovative information among partners. This requires prototyping "new mental models of the organization and its business," such as the model we have been outlining in this book.[10]

The old way of organizing pioneered by Ford and Sloan was based on an architecture of materials and not of the mind. Organizations in this mold had close spatial proximity and a strong organization working to hold them together and keep them on course. In the information age, the globally disaggregated, dynamic network form poses the question of how to keep things together psychologically while physically they are being radically dispersed. The cornerstones of contiguity and hierarchy are gone. In their place we must put knowledge management, personal recovery and health, vision, and spiritual identification. These elements form a new foundation for operations and make possible the continuously innovating company to which Brown refers.

Envisioning the World-Class Operations Center

The world-class operations center as we envision it has these major purposes:

- To identify the organization's core competencies and to form strategic alliances with others around the globe who can perform non-core activities better

- To serve as the primary arena of an organization's innovation

- To oversee all operations of the organization to make sure that they are in harmony with one another

- To establish and evaluate links to the organization's knowledge and learning dimension and to the centers of corporate strategic thinking or planning

With regard to the second purpose, the term *innovation* is used in its broadest possible sense, encompassing not only technological innovations related to products and services but also innovation in the manufacturing processes and structure of an organization. Thus, it involves conducting and evaluating experiments with regard to the performance of the organization's work. For instance, would workers function better in teams, and if so, what kinds of teams? It also involves developing prototypes and testing key innovations.

Organizations with world-class operations must have world-class information systems to monitor and control their global activities. The state of every node with respect to its activities and the resources it commands must be available on a regular, if not immediate, basis. This is needed to ensure harmonious functioning and adjusting among nodes as materials, energy, people, and information flow between them. While there are areas of overlap, the world-class operations center differs from the knowledge and learning center in that the former aggregates more detailed and highly specialized business information, while the latter aggregates and looks for broad patterns in the assumptions and interactions of key programs. To say it another way, while the operations center deals with the detailed knowledge necessary to develop and market new products, the learning and knowledge center is concerned with the highest-level assumptions of the organization in general, especially those that relate to its strategic future.

In parallel with the chief officers of the other centers, the head of the world-class operations center will perform a set of reviews and assessments. Her or his main concern is the continual reinvention of the company's manufacturing and production technologies. To this end, he or she will direct an internal research and development center that will come up with new products and services as well as new ways to manufacture, distribute, transport, and service them.

It is not only the new, entrepreneurial companies like those mentioned earlier that are benefiting from realigning their operations. Older companies—firms that were originally organized in the monolithic mode—are in the process of becoming dispersed, disaggregated, and networked. General Electric under the leadership of Jack Welch is a case in point.

General Electric has almost always been an international company. Formed in 1892 from Thomas Edison's old company, it soon began to work with Westinghouse, Siemans, and AEG in Europe to form a global oligopoly. After World War I, under the leadership of Gerard Swope, GE began to take active roles in Britain, Germany, France, Mexico, South Africa, Australia, and Japan. Following World War II, GE was among the first companies to sell patents to the Japanese and help them build new factories. The company became an unchallenged leader in a large number of markets in the United States, including those for industrial machinery, medical electronics, and consumer electronics. It also became stodgy, unwieldy, and sluggish. Vital information and management guidance had to slog through nearly twenty tiers in GE's hierarchical management structure just to reach the point where action could be taken.

During the 1980s, as the global business environment began to take form, CEO Jack Welch and his management team identified many problems with the company's strategy and structure and began to craft a new global plan. They decided to get out of any business, in any location, including the United States, in which GE could not attain a major competitive position worldwide, even if that business was currently profitable. As a result, GE underwent significant restructuring. It even sold off profitable U.S. businesses—including those related to small appliances and semiconductors—because it was not a strong competitor in those industries. In total, about $10 billion of business was jettisoned.

The corporation's investment portfolio was redirected and came to include interests in industrial robots and flexible manufacturing systems. Meanwhile, GE acquired several new businesses abroad, especially in Europe, in which management believed it could become a global leader. The total acquisition cost was about $19 billion and included the securities firm of Kidder, Peabody and the Tungsram lighting company of Hungary. Today, the GE label appears, for example, on microwave ovens designed, fabricated, and assembled by Sansung in South Korea. At the same time, the company has become the largest private employer in Singapore and is a major contributor to the Asian trading city's spectacular economic development. To carry out the new strategy, GE also had to streamline its management system.

As an editor at *Kiplinger's* put it, "Chief among GE's strategies is Welch's notion of a 'boundaryless' company that can do business in Cairo, Egypt, as easily as in Cairo, Ill."[11] Welch's vision is to blend the company together with its suppliers, customers, and other stakeholders into a global "seamless mass." His goal is to achieve not only faster but also higher-quality results and to match them more closely to GE customers' true needs.

The primary objective is to convert GE into a knowledge-based organization. GE's new strategy includes exploiting the company's informational and intellectual capital by means of worldwide diffusion and adaptation. It relies on a few core competencies that are centralized and many more unique competencies that are dispersed. Its worldwide activities adapt and leverage these competencies. Most of the company's knowledge base currently resides at the center in the United States and is transferred to overseas nodes where it may be adapted to local needs. The long-term strategy, however, is for each of its far-flung nodes to acquire new competencies that will be shared with other nodes throughout the world as GE evolves into a more fully networked form.

So far, Welch's strategy seems to be working. GE's worldwide revenues topped $58 billion in 1990. The company has had fifteen straight years of earnings-per-share growth and expects earnings to continue to grow. In 1991, GE had a total market value of over $67 billion, making it the fourth largest company in *Business Week*'s Global 1000, behind Nippon Telegraph & Telephone, Royal Dutch/Shell Group, and Exxon.

Coming Full Circle

With our discussion of the world-class operations dimension, we have come full circle. We have, in effect, challenged every one of the major assumptions underlying the design, operation, and maintenance of organizations in the past. We have seen that organizations, in order to function, require not only new concepts of information and knowledge but also a new structure for knowledge itself. We have also challenged the old psychological assumptions that undergird the way members of an organization have been managed, and in many cases, mismanaged. In addition, we have questioned the traditional assumption that the spiritual needs of the members of an organization are clearly separable from its mission. Finally, we have challenged the old assumption of centralized structure as the primary design principle of organizations.

Having all of its major assumptions questioned can be seen by an organization as either a threat or an opportunity. How such a challenge is perceived depends on the philosophy, health, spirit, and actions of an organization.

PART THREE

THE

NEW SPIRIT

OF BUSINESS

SEVEN

RADICAL STEPS
TOWARD A RADICAL
REDESIGN

"**B**usinessmen go down with their businesses because they like the old way so well they cannot bring themselves to change," wrote Henry Ford.[1] In this book we are prescribing radical change, and we have no illusions that such change will be easy, or even that managers will see it as desirable. It is human nature to have an emotional attachment to the status quo, even when our intellect tells us that clinging to it will lead to our demise. By the same token, organizations are strongly resistant to change and build the kinds of elaborate denial mechanisms we discussed in Chapter Four in order to avoid confronting the necessity of changing.

Steps to Total Ethical Management

Even if an organization does recognize the need for change, a purely cognitive approach is not enough. A viable approach to change must involve the emotions and the spirits of those affected as well. The twelve steps of Alcoholics Anonymous (AA) represent one—not the only—holistic approach. As we mentioned in Chapter Four, the twelve-step approach can be fruitfully extended to organizations themselves. We would like to propose here our own version of the twelve steps, describing the journey to a higher set of principles we call *total ethical management*.

Before we present our interpretation, though, it is critical to state an important qualification. The principles of AA are not to be viewed as abstract, theoretical propositions that are either strictly true or false and, hence, to be validated or invalidated by scientific means. Rather, they take on their full meaning only by being lived and, in many cases, by being discussed and interpreted daily within an ongoing group of people who are struggling to overcome the same problems.

Step One. "We admitted we were powerless over alcohol, that our lives had become unmanageable."[2] Translated into organizational terms, this first step of AA refers to the need for a brutally frank and courageous admission by top management that the principles by which they have managed their business thus far have led them or are leading them to failure. By whatever path management has traveled to reach the enlightened realization that they and their organization are out of control—most likely through the experience of a repeated series of major crises—management is finally able to admit that the principles they have used in the past to guarantee success are now responsible for imminent failure. Continued reliance on the old guarantors of success will in all probability lead to the organization's demise. The act of admitting that one's old principles were wrong is extremely difficult—all the more so since they were responsible for past success. Because of this, it is not an exaggeration to say that it is an act of extreme courage and heroism to admit that one is suffering from the failure of success—that what worked so well in the past is now responsible for failure. Notice that the first step is only an *admission* that the old business principles no longer work or guarantee success; it merely recognizes that management can no longer continue to *deny* the need for substantial change. This is the beginning of the transition from denial to rigorous honesty.

Step Two. "We came to believe that a Power greater than ourselves could restore us to sanity." As applied to an organization, the second step acknowledges the need for a higher set of ethical principles by which to judge and manage one's organization, and it expresses faith that such a set of principles exists. The new principles cannot be based on a slight extension or trivial modification of the old ones. While the "Power greater than ourselves" can obviously be interpreted as God, it need not be. What is required is the recognition that management must seek its new principles on an entirely different plane of reality. It has to leave the confines and the comfort of its old familiar moorings to venture out on a quest to totally unfamiliar lands.

The first and second steps of AA correspond in many

ways to the initial phases in the journey or the development of the hero described so well by Joseph Campbell.[3] The first step is not only the call to adventure, but a forceful call that can no longer be denied. If the hero denies the call, then he or she will not develop. The second step is the realization that the fledgling hero must break away almost completely from his or her old, familiar surroundings and journey out to a new environment if he or she is to develop. The development of the hero requires a quest.

The second step also recognizes that management is facing a crisis of values. It has lost sight of the fundamental purpose of business: to make quality products and to deliver quality services that satisfy the *ethical* desires and needs of humankind, not merely that which sells. Instead, the basis of the old set of management principles was immediate gratification, short-term gain, profit for the sake of profit. The second step acknowledges that there is another basis for existence. There is the recognition that spiritual emptiness is one of the prime sources of the organization's problems and that the organization can only be restored through submission to higher principles.

Step Three. "We made a decision to turn our will and our lives over to the care of God as we understood Him." For management, this third step of AA represents making an unbounded commitment to the new, higher set of principles which we call total ethical management. These principles have now been given top priority. In addition, the new principles are to be lived; they are for the purpose of changing how the organization acts, not merely how it thinks.

Step Four. "We made a searching and fearless moral inventory of ourselves." The fourth step is the first concrete act under the new principles. It consists of a brutally frank inventory conducted by top management of the organization's past "rights" and "wrongs" affecting itself or others. Not only are dysfunctional systems terribly hard on others, both physically and emotionally, but they are even harder, physically and emotionally, on themselves.) This moral inventory forms the basis for a redesign of the organization.

Step Five. "We admitted to God, to ourselves, and to another human being the exact nature of our wrongs." In terms of the organization, this step involves relatedness and confession to others regarding the organization's shortcomings. Step Five acknowledges that others must *participate actively* in the new design. They must not only critique the design but also participate in its development and execution.

If anything characterizes dysfunctional individuals and systems, it is their terrible isolation and loneliness; they are cut off not only from others but also from themselves. The fifth step thus recognizes that one's concept of a higher power, whatever it is, is a fundamental co-designer of the design.

Step Six. "We were entirely ready to have God remove all these defects of character." The organization is ready to implement a new design. Further, beyond readiness, top management has decided to place no roadblocks whatsoever in the way of implementing the new plan. Anyone who has ever worked with individuals or organizations in trouble knows that even though they have all kinds of good plans and intentions, very few of them are ever implemented or realized. In this step there is also the recognition that the design is to be driven by higher principles.

Step Seven. "We humbly asked Him to remove our shortcomings." With regard to the organization's new design, step seven further acknowledges the difficulty of implementation. It acknowledges that no matter how well top management has studied the original problem they faced, and admitted to organizational rights and wrongs, there is always doubt about whether the new plan is the right course of action. Since management has been wrong before, how can it be confident that it is right this time? No wonder humility is called for. Step seven thus says that management can go ahead and implement its plan but may not sweep its reservations completely away.

It is also important to acknowledge that unlike so many other programs for change, the twelve steps of AA underscore the concern regarding implementation. This emphasis is not overdone, since solutions to serious problems are not solutions at all unless implementation takes place.

Step Eight. "We made a list of all the persons we had harmed, and became willing to make amends to them." For the organization, step eight consists of taking an inventory of the stakeholders who have been harmed by the past actions of the organization. Management's willingness to make amends is the beginning of a process of reestablishing or rebuilding relations with others that have deteriorated as a result of the organization's dysfunction.

Step eight acknowledges that every plan, every action, no matter how good it appears, has harmful aspects. It forces management to look at the potentially harmful effects of new plans and to try to anticipate and remove them. It emphasizes the importance and the necessity of continually checking and rechecking plans.

Step Nine. "We made direct amends to such people wherever possible except when to do so would injure them or others." Step nine is another direct action step for the organization. It requires management to act on the inventory taken in step eight.

Step Ten. "We continued to take personal inventory and where we were wrong promptly admitted it." This step represents a commitment to a continuing moral audit. Management must institute an ongoing, permanent evaluation of the organizational system. Since the one thing that dysfunctional individuals and systems have strongly avoided in the past is an honest look at themselves, the twelve steps of AA are not content to leave evaluation to chance. Permanent, ongoing evaluation must be a central feature of the new management system.

Step Eleven. "We sought through prayer and meditation to improve our conscious contact with God as we understood Him, praying only for the knowledge of His will for us and the power to carry that out." The notions of prayer and meditation in step eleven are not to be taken literally, either by individuals or organizations. Prayer and meditation are only two examples of the immense number of ways (art, literature, poetry) that human beings have developed and exercised creativity. Step eleven is thus the realization of the need for continual creativity. Plans or new management principles are never finished. A permanent, ongoing relationship with a creative source is necessary.

Step Twelve. "Having had a spiritual awakening as a result of these steps, we try to carry these messages to alcoholics, and to practice these principles in all our affairs." Step twelve emphasizes the need to generalize the new, higher principles to as many other problems as possible. Indeed, step twelve forms the basis for the world service and spirituality dimension described in Chapter Five. Step twelve expresses management's commitment to the design of a completely different organization.

Step twelve can also be construed as indicating the need to return to step one, to continually reassess the new principles. Management came to step one in the first place because it was not sufficiently proactive or anticipatory of problems in the past; it failed in the past to be sufficiently critical and aware of the principles that undergirded its actions. Step twelve says that management can no longer afford to act in this way. The more that management believes that the new system is the answer or is working well, the more management needs to be critical of it and to carry it through all of the twelve steps.

EIGHT

TOTAL
ETHICAL
MANAGEMENT

Throughout this book, we have been approaching, step-by-step, a new concept of management. This new concept underlies and ties together everything we have articulated. We call it total ethical management. It provides a needed philosophical foundation for the functions and structure of business we have outlined.

In this final chapter, we explore the principles that define total ethical management and that will guide the organizations of the future. We discuss how these principles will look in practice when they are applied to the leadership of complex organizations. They are the principles that undergird the twelve-step approach to the radical change needed for the realization of total ethical management and the survival of organizations.

New Principles for Management

The basic principle of total ethical management is that organizations exist fundamentally to serve people—if not all of humanity—and not the other way around. Those organizations that lose sight of this basic principle forfeit not only their legitimacy but their fundamental right to exist. The organizations of the nineteenth and twentieth centuries are obsolete because they fail to serve humanity's broader purposes and at the same time are less able to achieve even their own narrow goals.

The principle that every business is, or should be, in the service of humanity broadens the scope of an organization's concerns and necessitates the new functions and structures we have proposed. This can be seen by examining the principle's corollaries:

- *Organizations have a fundamental moral and ethical responsibility to treat employees as whole human beings.* This means recognizing their emotional complexity and spiritual impulses as well as their cognitive needs. This principle is embodied in the knowledge and learning, recovery and development, and world service and spirituality dimensions we have described.

- *Organizations have a fundamental moral and ethical responsibility to make quality products and deliver quality services that meet real needs.* Thus, the primary goal is serving humankind, not just purveying that which sells. Meeting consumer needs at the highest level of quality is the ultimate purpose of total quality management. (Note carefully that total *quality* management is not the same as total *ethical* management, which is broader both in spirit and concept.)

- *Organizations have a fundamental moral and ethical responsibility to get their products and services to all who are in ethical need of them.* Despite all the abundance in the world, the basic needs of the vast majority of humankind are barely satisfied. Satisfying these needs is the ultimate purpose of world-class operations as well as the function of globalism.

- *Organizations have a fundamental moral and ethical responsibility to control technology in the service of the social and environmental good.* Industrial accidents like those at Bhopal and Chernobyl and the Exxon Valdez oil spill should not and need not happen. The ultimate purpose of environmentalism and crisis management is to identify major social and environmental risks posed by technology and to manage or control them, if not prevent them altogether.

- *Organizations have a fundamental moral and ethical responsibility to aid and serve future generations.* Where business, science, and the intellect generally tell us to limit or terminate our concern for future generations, the ethics and issues management functions tell us to extend our concern for unborn generations as far into the future as we can possibly imagine, and beyond. Where conventional business and economic reasoning tells us that the present value of future generations is virtually nil, or becomes nil the farther a generation is removed from us, spirituality and ethics insist that future generations are at least as important as we are. There is no temporal limit to caring. Or put differently, there is no "discount rate" for caring, as there apparently is for future generations considered only in conventional economic terms— that is, as investments.

Of all the organizations with which we are familiar, none comes as close to total ethical management as the Body Shop. Its principles, which we have listed below, are strikingly similar to those we have just listed.

1. The Body Shop's goals and values are as important as our products and our profits.

2. Our policies and our products are geared to meet the real needs of real people, both inside and outside the company.

3. Honesty, integrity, and caring form the foundations of the company, and should flow through everything we do.

4. We care about each other as individuals; we will continue to endeavor to bring meaning and pleasure to the workplace.

5. We care about our customers, and will continue to bring humanity into the marketplace.

6. We care about humanizing the business community;
    we will continue to show that success and profits
    can go hand in hand with ideals and values.

7. We will demonstrate our care for the world in which
    we live, by respecting fellow human beings, by not
    harming animals, by working to conserve our planet.

8. We will continue to create products that show that
    we care, by not testing on animals, by using naturally
    based ingredients that are close to source, by making
    products which work for our customers.

9. We will continue to search, to challenge, to question,
    to celebrate life and generate joy and excitement.

10. We embrace everyone who works for The Body Shop
    and with The Body Shop as part of our extended fam-
    ily. We are all the Company; it is up to all of us to
    make it work.[1]

A New Practice of Leadership

Total ethical management will be the central integrating
philosophy of leadership in the organization of the future.
A leadership team composed of the top officers of the organization, plus the heads of the four special centers, will
collectively oversee the different parts of the organization.
The team's primary task will be to maintain the wisdom of
the whole.

Wisdom is not only the essence of leadership but also

the special requirement of leadership in the organization of the future. Wisdom unites knowledge with action. It depends on three capabilities:

- Holistic thinking: the ability to view an organization in its entirety

- Reflectiveness: the ability to critically examine oneself

- Judgment: the power to understand, compare, weigh, and decide in a manner that is sound and serene

Most important, wisdom requires an understanding of the organization and its mission as a whole. Wise leadership is achieved by remaining aware of the whole, not by overanalyzing or overcontrolling any of its parts.

The wisdom of the whole is informed by the activities of the four dimensions we have described, each of which pursues a different ideal.

- The knowledge and learning dimension pursues the ideal of truth. Its quest is for the kind of knowledge that will enable us to manage complex systems.

- The recovery and development dimension pursues the ideal of goodness. Its quest is for individual and organizational health.

- The world service and spirituality dimension pursues the ideal of beauty. Its quest is for a world in which there is harmony with nature and within humanity.

- The world-class operations dimension pursues the ideal of pragmatism. Its quest is to manufacture products or render services that make an ethical difference in human lives.

Leadership looks for and manages the natural synergy and conflict within these four dimensions. Every organization struggles every day with the tension between getting new products and services out the door (operations) and respecting the emotional and spiritual needs and health of its members. Three conflicts between the various dimensions are especially important to note: (1) emotional health versus operations, (2) spiritual service versus operations, and (3) knowledge versus operations. The first and third conflicts are ones that have traditionally stymied organizations. In addition, the design we have outlined throughout this book introduces a new one: the conflict between service and operations. Leadership makes these tensions explicit and works to resolve them.

The conflicts among the four dimensions are balanced by their synergy. When an organization has a spiritual vision that touches the most deeply held values of all of its members, employees are motivated to perform, benefiting world-class operations. The permanent, ongoing, intensive treatment provided by the recovery and development dimension enables employees to maintain health and productivity in the face of stress caused by rapid change and the complexity of global operations. And the knowledge and learning dimension coordinates important interactions among the organization's far-flung operations. Leadership recognizes and encourages such synergy.

While the leadership team oversees synergy and conflict, it also creates an inspiring vision and issues guidelines and plans that are open to discretionary interpretation by the operating units. It strives to encourage decision making at lower levels of the organization by distributing power and authority where it can be employed effectively to respond to the demands of a rapidly changing environment. *Fortune* presents Jack Welch, CEO of GE, as a model: "The scrappy CEO has mounted a radical assault on the canons of modern management—which GE largely wrote. 'We've got to take out the boss element,' Welch says. By his lights, 21st-century managers will forgo their old powers—to plan, organize, implement, and measure—for new duties: counselling groups, providing resources for them, helping them think for themselves. 'We're going to win on our ideas,' he says, 'not by whips and chains.' "[2]

Paul Allaire of Xerox employs a similar strategy. He says to the line manager, "You cannot do to your people what was done to you. You have to be a facilitator or a coach, and, by the way, we're still going to hold you to the bottom line."[3] While empowering decision making lower in the organization, Allaire also recognizes the importance of maintaining the wisdom of the whole: "We have put a decision-making process in place that will directly involve the line managers of the business divisions. Of course, they will have to make compromises at times. There may well be an optimum technology for one division and a very different one for another. Since we can't afford to develop both, we will have to sit down and say, 'What is the right technology for Xerox as a whole?' "[4]

To develop future leaders as well as its current members,

the leadership team will seek to nourish and stimulate the qualities of leadership described by Warren Bennis in his book *On Becoming a Leader*. Drawing on the numerous interviews he has conducted, as well as the extensive literature, Bennis observes that leaders have mastered four fundamental arts: (1) becoming self-expressive, (2) listening to one's inner voice, (3) learning from the appropriate mentors, and (4) giving oneself over to a guiding vision.[5] In addition to a guiding vision, leaders possess such attributes as passion, integrity, trust, curiosity, and daring, writes Bennis.[6]

Jack Welch of GE and Paul Allaire of Xerox demonstrate some of the key characteristics of leadership as it will be practiced in the organizations of the future. They have distributed power and decision making throughout their organizations while retaining responsibility for the whole. They have decided the problems to which the divisions of their companies should attend. They have sought to drive out complacency by examining assumptions and continually asking *why* questions. They have sought stability when it was appropriate. And most importantly, they have summoned the courage to change when it was needed.

The Need for Change in Business Schools

Finally, we must note that American business schools are just as responsible for the trouble that American business is in as the businesses themselves. We would be derelict in our assessment of the organizations of the future if we were not also critical of academic institutions. Those of us in the academic community cannot in good conscience ask businesses to change their structures in order to respond to the extreme challenges of the new world and yet contend that the structures of business schools do not also need to change radically.

Business schools are still largely organized around the traditional functions of accounting, finance, and so forth. As we have noted repeatedly, these traditional functions, although they do have a place, are no longer the fundamental building blocks of business education and knowledge. The dominance of the traditional functions means that the new functions we have identified will be dealt with, at best, on the periphery of the business school curriculum. They will not be accorded the center stage we believe they now deserve.

Like business itself, business schools have responded to the new challenges with quick fixes. If they even acknowledge the new problems, they merely insert mention of them into the study of traditional functions. In short, the old functions still dominate. Whatever the new designs for businesses and business schools ultimately turn out to be, they must be holistic. They must recognize the interconnectedness of the different types of knowledge needed to manage organizations. We can no longer afford businesses—or business schools—that are reductionist.

Final Remarks

Total ethical management is not yet a full-blown entity. No organization, to our knowledge, has fully embraced the concept of total ethical management or the new structure and functions described in this book. Yet, as the preceding chapters have shown, many have incorporated significant parts of them.

It is not our desire that every or even any organization implement the exact structure and functions that we have described. Rather, we have attempted to lay out a broad general framework and a set of concerns that are based on solid underlying logic. Ultimately, the concerns we have raised must be addressed by organizations that want to be effective in the future.

Total ethical management is an idea whose time has come. Striving to realize it can give us the means and the hope to continue the struggle to make our organizations and ourselves more fully human.

NOTES

Chapter One

1. John Greenwald, "What Went Wrong?" *Time*, Nov. 9, 1992, pp. 45-50.
2. Gary Jacobson and John Hillkirk, *Xerox: American Samurai* (New York: Macmillan, 1986), 8.
3. Quotes from Paul Allaire in this section are from Robert Howard, "The CEO Is Organizational Architecture: An Interview with Xerox's Paul Allaire," *Harvard Business Review*, Sept.-Oct. 1992, p. 108.
4. Alfred D. Chandler, Jr., *Scale and Scope* (Cambridge, Mass.: Belknap Press of Harvard University, 1990).
5. Oliver E. Williamson, *Markets and Hierarchies* (New York: Free Press, 1975).
6. Ricardo Semler, "Managing Without Managers: How One Unorthodox Company Makes Money by Avoiding Decisions, Rules, and Executive Authority," *Harvard Business Review*, Sept.-Oct. 1989, pp. 73-83.

7. A. L. Brian, "Chaparral Steel: Unleash Workers and Cut Costs," *Fortune*, May 18, 1992, p. 88.

Chapter Two

1. Hector Tobar, "Family Seeks Ten Million for Injury at McDonald's Playland," *Los Angeles Times*, Nov. 6, 1991, pp. A-3, A-19.

2. Sharon Bernstein, "Advocates for Children's TV Air Their Beef with McDonald's," *Los Angeles Times*, Dec. 20, 1991, p. F-6.

3. See Walter P. von Wartburg, "Political Issue Management with Common Sense," *Industrial Crisis Quarterly*, 1989, *3*(4), 303–318.

4. See Christine M. Pearson and Ian I. Mitroff, "From Crisis Prone to Crisis Prepared: A Framework for Crisis Management," *The Executive*, 1993, *7*(1), 48–59; see also Thierry C. Pauchant and Ian I. Mitroff, *Transforming the Crisis-Prone Organization: Preventing Individual, Organizational, and Environmental Tragedies* (San Francisco: Jossey-Bass, 1992).

5. See W. Edwards Deming, *Out of the Crisis* (Cambridge, Mass.: MIT Center for Advanced Engineering Study, 1982); see also J. M. Juran, *Juran on Planning for Quality* (New York: Free Press, 1988).

6. James O'Toole, "Do Good, Do Well: The Business Enterprise Trust Awards," *California Management Review*, 1991, *33*(3), 21–22.

7. Emily T. Smith, "Doing It for Mother Earth: How to Cut Pollution, Please Regulators—and Save Money," *Business Week*, Oct. 25, 1991, pp. 44, 46.

8. See Jay R. Galbraith, Edward E. Lawler III, and Associates, *Organizing for the Future: The New Logic for Managing Complex Organizations* (San Francisco: Jossey-Bass, 1993).

Chapter Three

1. This example is taken from Pauchant and Mitroff, *Transforming the Crisis-Prone Organization*.

2. See Richard O. Mason and Ian I. Mitroff, *Challenging Strategic Planning Assumptions* (New York: John Wiley, 1981) for a detailed explanation of how this process works.

3. See James Bryan Quinn, "The Intelligent Enterprise: A New Paradigm," *The Executive*, Nov. 1992, pp. 48–63; see also C. West Churchman, *The Design of Inquiring Systems* (New York: Basic Books, 1971). Churchman's pioneering work in philosophy, management, and social science is one of the roots of our concept of the knowledge and learning dimension.

4. See Ian I. Mitroff and Harold Linstone, *The Unbounded Mind* (New York: Oxford University Press, 1993).

5. This example is taken from Solveig Wikstrom, "The Customer as Co-Producer," paper presented at the Twelfth Annual International Conference of the

Strategic Management Science Society, London, England, 1992.

6. See Ian I. Mitroff, Richard O. Mason, and Vincent P. Barabba, *The 1980 Census: Policy Making Amid Turbulence* (Lexington, Mass.: Lexington Books, 1983).

7. Gerald Zaltman and Vincent P. Barabba, *Hearing the Voice of the Market* (Cambridge, Mass.: Harvard Business School Press, 1991), 38, 39. In their book, Zaltman and Barabba develop the notion of a chief information officer that is very close to the one we propose.

8. Zaltman and Barabba, *Hearing the Voice*, 50-51.

Chapter Four

1. Jan Larson, "Treating the Whole Person at Westinghouse," *American Demographics*, June 1991, pp. 32-33.

2. Jan Halper, *Quiet Desperation: The Truth About Successful Men* (New York: Warner Books, 1988), 86.

3. David Gelman and Caroline Friday, "Overstressed by Success: For Scores of CEOs, It's Terrifying at the Top," *Newsweek*, June 3, 1991, p. 56.

4. Douglas LaBier, *Modern Madness: The Emotional Fallout of Success* (Menlo Park, Calif.: Addison-Wesley, 1986).

5. Manfred F. R. Kets de Vries and Associates (eds.), *Organizations on the Couch: Clinical Perspectives on*

Organizational Behavior and Change (San Francisco: Jossey-Bass, 1991).

6. See Anne Wilson Schaef and Diane Fassel, *The Addictive Organization: Why We Overwork, Cover Up, Pick Up the Pieces, Please the Boss, and Perpetuate Sick Organizations* (New York: HarperCollins, 1988); see also Mary Riley, *Corporate Healing: Solutions to the Impact of the Addictive Personality in the Workplace* (Deerfield Beach, Fla.: Health Communications, 1990).

7. See Robert H. Rosen, *The Healthy Company* (Los Angeles: Tarcher, 1991).

8. Pearson and Mitroff, "From Crisis Prone to Crisis Prepared," 48–59.

9. See Pauchant and Mitroff, *Transforming the Crisis-Prone Organization*.

10. For an introduction to the vast literature on organizational culture, see Ralph H. Kilmann, *Beyond the Quick Fix: Managing Five Tracks to Organizational Success* (San Francisco: Jossey-Bass, 1984); Edgar H. Schein, *Organizational Culture and Leadership*, 2nd ed. (San Francisco: Jossey-Bass, 1992).

11. C. West Churchman was one of the first philosopher-planners to reinterpret the principles of Alcoholics Anonymous in terms of their relevance to organizations. See C. West Churchman and Ian I. Mitroff, *In the Service of Humanity*, manuscript in preparation, 1993; see also Lee Robbins, "Designing More Functional Organizations: The Twelve-Step Model," *Jour-*

nal of Organizational Change Management, 1993,
5(4), 58.

12. Larson, "Treating the Whole Person," p. 32.

Chapter Five

1. Beverly Byette, "Veggie Philanthropist, Charity: Mickey Weiss Helps Feed Hundreds of Thousands of Hungry People in the Southland by Salvaging Millions of Pounds of Unsaleable but Perfectly Edible Produce That Used to Be Thrown Away," *Los Angeles Times*, Oct. 25, 1989, p. E-1.

2. In personal communication with C. West Churchman.

3. See, for instance, Frederick Turner, "Natural Technology," unpublished paper, University of Texas at Dallas, Richardson, Texas, 1990.

4. See William James, *Pragmatism* (Buffalo, N.Y.: Prometheus Books, 1991), 127; see also Patrick K. Dooley, *Pragmatism as Humanism: The Philosophy of William James* (Chicago: Nelson-Hall, 1974), 155–156.

5. Ian I. Mitroff and Thierry C. Pauchant, *We're So Big and Powerful Nothing Bad Can Happen to Us: An Investigation of America's Crisis-Prone Corporations* (New York: Birch Lane Press, 1990).

6. Edgar A. Singer, Jr., "Mechanism, Vitalism, Naturalism: A Logico-Historical Study," *Philosophy of Science*, 1946, *13*(2), 81–99.

7. William James, *The Varieties of Religious Experience:*

A Study in Human Nature (New York: Macmillan, 1961), 110–111.

8. David Ferrell, "Cafe Installs Doomsday Clock," *Los Angeles Times*, Jan. 31, 1992, pp. B-1, B-2.

Chapter Six

1. Allan Nevins and Frank Ernest Hill, *Ford: Expansion and Challenge 1915–33* (New York: Scribner's, 1957), 257.

2. Robert B. Reich, *The Work of Nations* (New York: Knopf, 1991), 112.

3. Burt Nanus, *Visionary Leadership: Creating a Compelling Sense of Direction for Your Corporation* (San Francisco: Jossey-Bass, 1992), 8.

4. Oliver E. Williamson, *Markets and Hierarchies* (New York: Free Press, 1975).

5. Reich, *The Work of Nations*, 113.

6. "Sun Is Shining—With a Lot of Help from Its Friends," *Business Week*, Nov. 23, 1992, pp. 92–93.

7. Hal F. Rosenbluth, *The Customer Comes Second and Other Secrets of Exceptional Service* (New York: William Morrow, 1992), and personal interviews with David Miller, Vice President for Global Information Technology, Rosenbluth Travel.

8. "Research That Reinvents the Corporation," *Harvard Business Review*, Jan.–Feb. 1991, p. 102.

9. "Research That Reinvents the Corporation," 108.

10. "Research That Reinvents the Corporation," 104.

11. *Kiplinger's*, Aug. 1991, p. 22.

Chapter Seven

1. Henry Ford and Samuel Crowther, *My Life and Work* (Salem, N.H.: Ayer, 1922), 43.
2. This and the other eleven steps quoted are from Alcoholics Anonymous World Services, 1957; the interpretation of the steps developed here is based on extensive personal communication and discussion with C. West Churchman.
3. Joseph Campbell, *The Hero with a Thousand Faces*, Bollingen Series 15 (Princeton, N.J.: Princeton University Press, 1949).

Chapter Eight

1. Quoted in Birgitta Schwartz, "The Body Shop: The Environment as a Mission," unpublished paper, Gothenburg Research Institute, University of Gothenburg, Gothenburg, Sweden, 1992, pp. 19–20.
2. Thomas A. Stewart, "GE Keeps Those Ideas Coming, It Wrote the Book on Management. Now Jack Welch Is Rewriting It—To Tap Employees' Brain Power," *Fortune*, Aug. 12, 1991, pp. 41–42.
3. Robert Howard, "The CEO Is Organizational Architecture: An Interview with Xerox's Paul Allaire," *Harvard Business Review*, Sept.–Oct. 1992, p. 108.
4. Howard, "The CEO Is Organizational Architecture," 108.

5. Warren Bennis, *On Becoming a Leader* (Menlo Park, Calif.: Addison-Wesley, 1989), 34.

6. Bennis, *On Becoming a Leader*, 34.

INDEX

Semco (Brazilian manufacturing company), 11-12
Sexual harassment, 62
Singer, E. A., 88-89
Sloan, A. P., 99, 112
Sourcing, 105
Spirituality: acknowledgement and expression of, 33, 81-89; environmental movement as, 84; free will versus determinism debate in, 85-86; and structural theories of organizations, 88. *See also* World service
Strategic alliances: and global web, 106; versus ownership, 104-105; sourcing and outsourcing in, 105; and systemic view, 45; and trend tracking, 22
Stress, and encore anxiety, 59-60
Structural theories of organizational behavior, 88
Sun Microsystems, 106-107
Swope, G., 115

T

Technology, employee development of, 12
Total ethical management, 129-139; four dimensions of, 134-135; leadership team in, 133-137; principles, corollaries to, 130-133; principles, twelve-step, 122-128
Total quality management (TQM), 23, 45; and environmentalism, 26-27; and ethics, 27; and globalism, 27
Total systems approach: and crisis management, 22-23; environmentalism in, 24,

30-31; global strategy in, 25, 31-32; interrelated functions in, 26-32; new corporate functions in, 20-25, 30; structure in, 32-36; and total quality management, 23
Trend tracking, critical priority of, 21-22
Twelve-step proposal, 122-128

U

University of Southern California Center for Crisis Management, 30

V

Value chain: activities in, 102-103; disaggregated, 104-105, 107-110
Vision, corporate, 101-103
Volvo, 46

W

Weiss, M., 78-80
Welch, J., 115-117, 136
Westinghouse, 75
Williamson, O., 105
Wisdom, as essence of leadership, 133-134
World-class operations, 33-34, 101-113, 131; disaggregated value chain in, 104-105, 107-110; and innovative information exchange, 112; and organizational fission, 103-113; strategic alliances in, 104-110; and vision, 101-102

World-class operations center,
113-117; chief officers of,
114-115
World service, 33, 93-95.
See also Spirituality
World service and spirituality
center, 90-92; chief officer's
role in, 92

X

Xerox: reorganization of, 4-7;
and technology, 136

Z

Zaltman, G., 50-52